EAGLE EATS JAGUAR'S HEART

TOME 4: THE COMING OUT

Illustrations and story by

c. huilo c.

A Jaguar Moon Press Book

all type and design by
Jaguarlunart productions
All illustrations and story by c. huilo c.
Photographs by c. huilo c.

For more info visit:
www.jaguarlunart.com
www.jaguarmoonpress.com
www.deep-woods-art.com

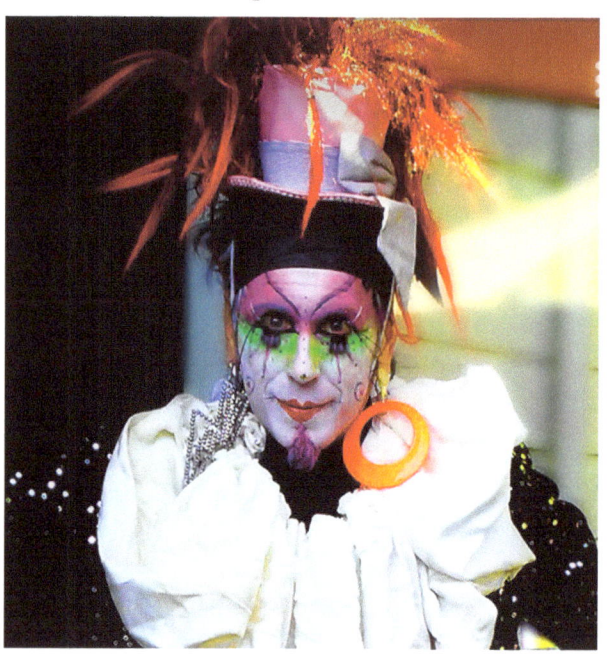

ISBN: 9780985487867
Library of Congress Control Number: 2018942746
Other books in Tales of a Jaguar Magicians series:
Flight of the Jaguar Magician v3 PCN 2018942748   ISBN 9780985487836
Marriage of Moon & Jaguar v2 PCN 2018942748   ISBN 9780985487850
Vibration of Hummingbird   PCN 2018942748   ISBN 9780985487874
Tales of a Jaguar Magician   PCN 2018942745   ISBN 9780985487881

Visit www.jaguarlunart.com and www.jaguarmoonpress.com to order additional copies.

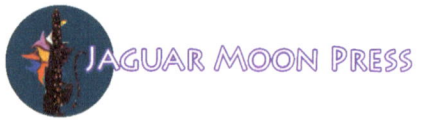
JAGUAR MOON PRESS

FORWARD

*M*any moons passed since the Creators had conjured dear Lola, the effervescent Jaguar Magician. Since wedding the magic with Luna, Lola was called forth into a deeper level of experience. Indeed, the question of "Who am I?" had propelled Lola through some of the wildest examinations of consciousness. Lola's quest to awaken other Jaguar Magicians, had led heshe through trials with passion, with ego, and quite simply all the foibles that humanity could encounter—almost.

After the Marriage of the Moon & Jaguar, it became clear that in order for Lola to do their work, they must experience in person the entirety of the 3-D fixed-state realm on the Planet of Great Consciousness. By doing so, Lola would be able to sense distinctly what may help activate the waning of wonder and curiosity within the jaguar magicians. Not only lifting the levels of magical remembrance for gender fluid beings, Lola also aspired to help liberate and release the dense cloak of delusion that masked the entire realm of Gaia.

Lola's teacher, Ocelotl, at the request of the Aguila Phoenis, promised there would be minimal intervention while heshe went about their quest. They both knew that the 3-D realm would likely be tricky for Lola, however they hoped it would open heshe's heart and deepen their empathic capacity and expand the flow of compassion. Humanos in the realm of Gaia had been interfered with on their course of evolushun for millennia and it was time for the exploiters to release them from forbidden control and instead, help them step into their greater truth.

With the magical tools acquired during Lola's passage through the mirrors and the lattice, it seemed that heshe would be ready to transmute some of the crisis situations on the blue planeta. As Lola prepared to enter the portal via the Ojo Siempretis' Entrada de Finitum, the Planet of Great Consciousness continued to be rattled by fears and destruction.

The exposure to commodified behaviors, the horrific levels of trash and the general disruption was about to be faced head-on by Lola. Magical new friends, including Grass Hoppre, Dev Lish, Ratita, Fractal Chick and many more await Lola's passage. Each new character illumines Lola on how to traverse the 3-D realm in the best way possible.

So now, let's join Lola with coming out into 3-D and see how heshe liberates others on the journey for transcending humanos into 5-D consciousness. As each queerly gendered being practiced a ritual of "coming out", so too, was it time for Lola to emerge from the veil of the cloak of innoncence that surrouned heshe. Come out! Come out! Lola, the 3-D realms await your magic...

TOME 4

THE
COMING
OUT

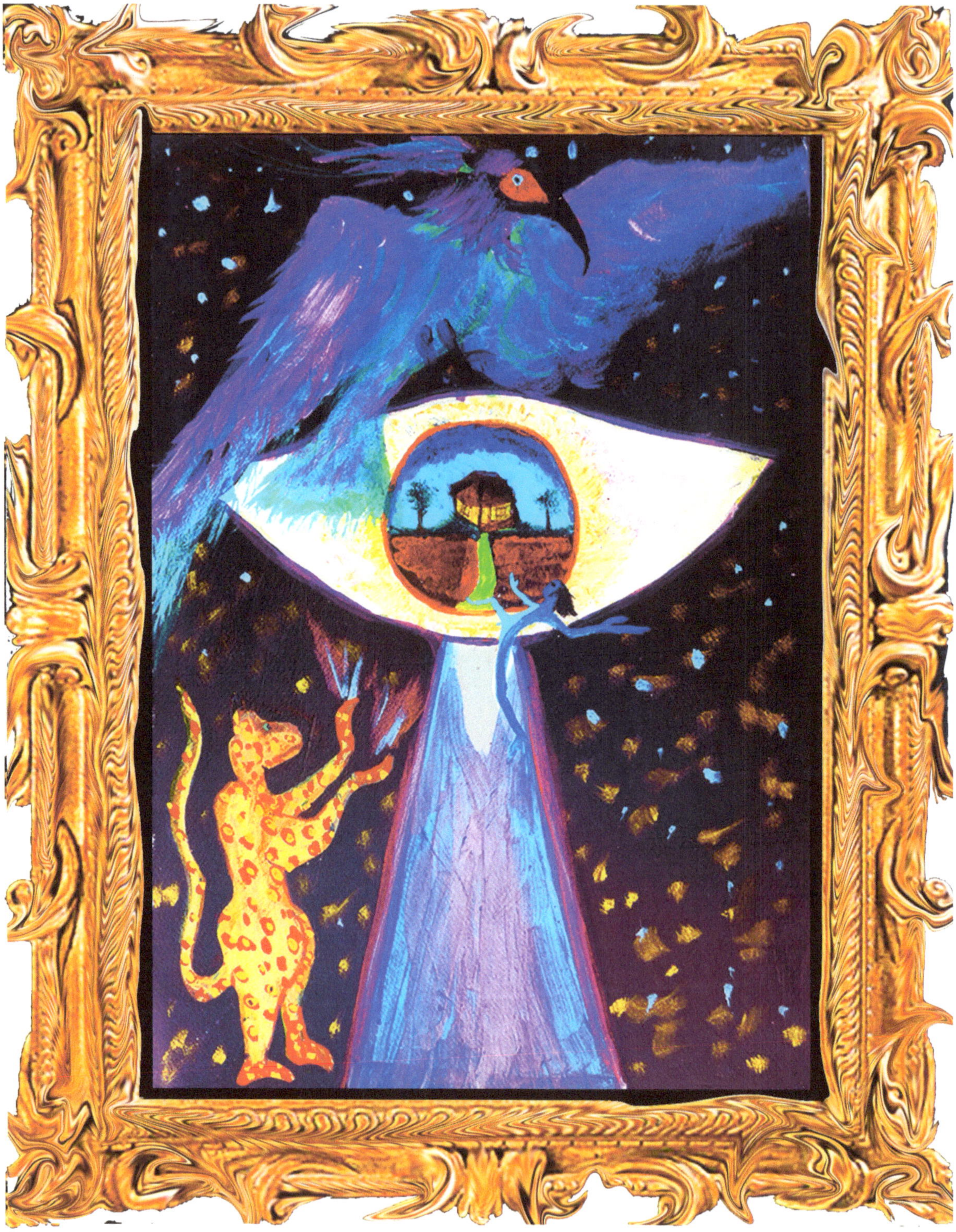

*O*celotl gathered with Phoenix and waited for Lola to join them. "It seems this is going to be a major turning point for Lola. From naïve student to wisdom-keeper."

"Greetings everyone! I'm ready to leap forward." Lola enthusiastically pointed toward the majestic Eye.

"Indeed, I bet you are, but Lola do you know why we are sending you? It is because we feel that when you are actually in the 3-D spectrum, feeling it in every way, then the experience will guide you to true liberation. That freedom will mirror back ten-fold to the others in the Planet of Great Consciousness. Now remember, we are always with you. The 3-D world has severe tensions that seem real, yet in reality they are dreams and you have the power to restructure them. Do you have any questions or concerns," asked Ocelotl?

"Not really. You have taught me much. I am ready and willing. Shall I begin?" Even though Lola had been through so much and gathered important skills, heshe was still curious and hopeful about entering the full spectrum of the 3-D humano experience. Lola waved goodbye to heshe's allies and triumphantly wandered into the giant iris of the All-Seeing-All-Knowing-Eye. Once through the vortex heshe came upon a bright green path which lead deeper into the 3-D world. On the horizon Lola saw a glowing golden house. Heshe hummed a little tune to help guide the way.

Off I go on the path forward
Wandering into the eye of the unknown
Oh how I have grown
The path forward into 3-D
To remember this I am filled with glee
What will I see?
How will it change me?
Following my intuition
Let it reveal thy information!

*I*ndeed, springing forward seemed effortless. Passing through the giant iris was immediate and without any interruption. Lola turned back a second time but heshe's friends were no longer in sight. There was a pop and a loud crack and then a swift puff of wind. Now, Lola stood on a vibrant emerald pathway and began to walk towards the only building on the horizon. Perhaps someone there could share ideas on where they should go next? While walking, Lola came upon a verdant, stately tree. Not sure if things could hear the same way as in heshe's other world, yet Lola to the tree, "Hello good being. I am Lola from the Selva and friends of Ocelotl's and the Phoenix. I have come

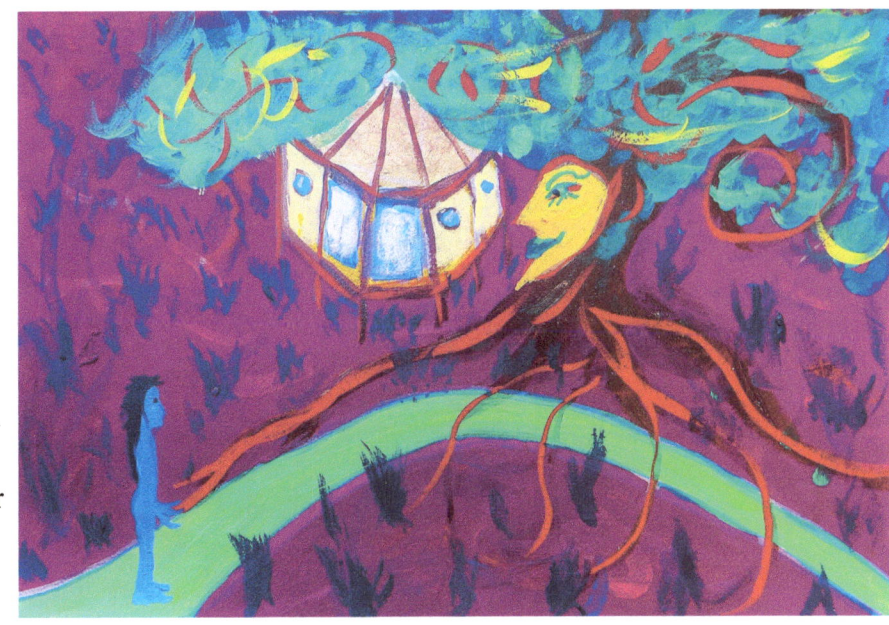

to learn about the 3-D world. Can you help guide me?"

The tree shook a bit, as if it had been sleeping. A face appeared on the trunk and produced a wide smile. "Oh my! No one has talked to me for so long… well, except for Magian Purpol. You say are from the other realms? Welcome!" The tree waved its branches. "We are here to guide you, those of us whom still exist anyway. Sadly, some of my family have been tortured in the 3-D spectrum. Well then, you asked could I possibly guide you? What do you mean by that? Where to go?"

"Why yes, I haven't a clue where to go or who to see or what to know? I am so curious," stated Lola. Heshe walked forward to gently hold one of the branches on the tree.

"Ah well, then, I think it may be best to speak with the Magian, Purpol. He lives in that golden house. Although, he normally doesn't come out until night you can wait here and have some of my fruit. These are manzanas. Let them nourish you on your journey. And remember, keep your roots to the ground. It is important to maintain your origins deep in the nourishment of the soil."

Lola sat next to the tree and delighted in the sumptuous fruit the tree had generously offered.

The sky turned violet and stars began to shimmer. Lola was getting restless to meet his first guide, Magian Purpol. Heshe wondered if knocking on the door was polite? But, just then, heshe heard the door creak open and out walked a short man in violet robes.

"Lola, thank you for waiting, I was traveling and just arrived back. The tree has shared you would like suggestions on where to go," queried the magician?

"I would. So, if you wouldn't mind?" Lola approached the house.

"Well good then. Step up here and we'll give the house a twirl. You haven't completely entered the 3-D world although, you are very near. This is a sort of betwixt the worlds place where one can select a

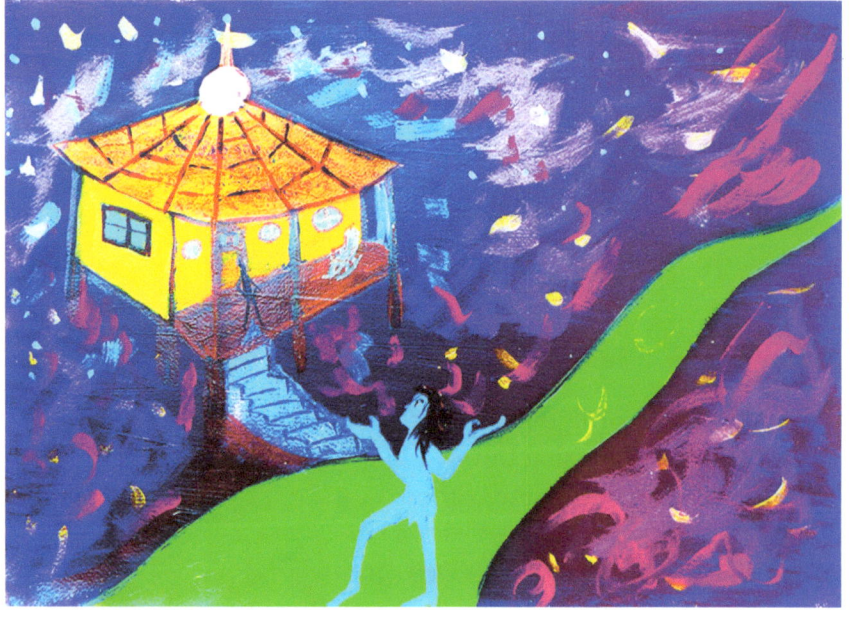

'filter' for how you will witness the world of Gaia. I am the guardian of windows and doors. I hold the keys of perspective. There are so many ways to view the world, different lenses, if you will. You see, each humano has an agreement of sorts with its oversoul for karmic and soul evolution work they desire to fulfill or participate in… it's not all willy nilly!"

"Ah, OK, so there is choice to the humanos situations," asked Lola?

"Indeed! Humanos are sets of starseeds. Coming from various dimensions and genetic makings, yet when they enter 3-D most of this is erased from the surface of their memories. They can spend lifetimes retrieving it or never remembering it until they die and transform. However, it is a time of quickening on the planet so more starseeds are arriving ready to be awakened." Purpol cleared his throat. "Anyway, these facial screens are somewhat different from the wizarding masks where you came from on the planeta. These are filters to enhance or clarify—even direct a view—hence personal experience. So why don't you step inside and join me. We'll see what the house recommends for you and I'll show you some of the selves others have selected.

*L*ola had been inside many strange places, but this one was very different. It sort of reminded heshe of the House of Many Selves. Inside, there were numerous doors and windows, but no furniture, nothing else to distract the mind.

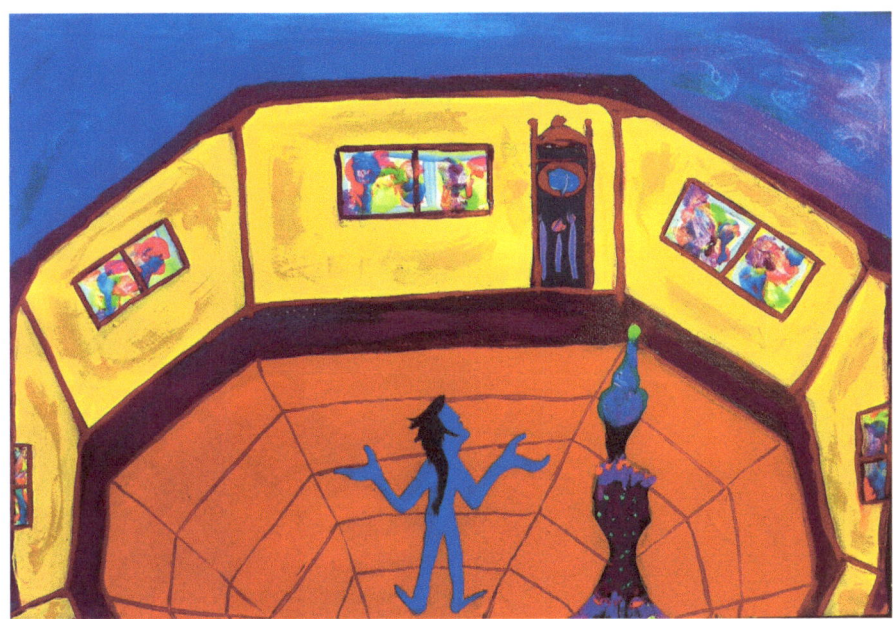

"There are eight sides to this house. It represents infinite possibilities. You can open a door, then we turn the house and the same door will have a different view. Would you like to try?"

"How do you turn the house," inquired Lola?

"Ahahaha! Good questions. Like this!" Purpol snapped his fingers and the house jolted forward and spun slowly. "We can do it faster if you'd like. Do you get motion sickness?"

"Uh, no, I don't think so." Lola walked up to a window with Purpol.

The windows were glass yet the view was smoky and unclear. Purpol reached out and touched a window and in a few moments, it became clear. Together they stood looking out onto the horizon and saw Ocelotl, the Phoenix and the All-Seeing-All-Knowing-Eye.

"Wow, What's that? I don't want to go back yet," exclaimed Lola.

"No, no, no. It's just to show you that you can always and will always be able to return home to the domain of benevolent source. Just know that inside, as it will come in handy. Now, let's give it a whirl and see what the other portals have in store!"

*I*n a moment, there were eyes, eyes, and more eyes. They began to glow and float inside the window. Purpol reached out and caught one.

"This is more than just any ole eye. This is the empathic eye. It is an emotive filter many choose so they can feel what they see. With this path the evolutionary challenge is to increase empathy into a state of compassion. Sometimes, though with this type of filter, humanos can almost feel too much. It may lead to apathy, or even depression."

Purpol examined the eye more closely. "You see, the eye responds to everything that enters the vibrational field through motion and color. It interprets this based on experience or divine memory and projects images for the mind to respond to and the body creates enzymes and such to subsequently perform tasks. The eye is such a revered source."

"I certainly understand due to my time with the All-Seeing-All-Knowing-Eye. Isn't it true this connects to the pineal? Would it also help one with relationship of relaxing the 'fixed' nature of 3-D?" Lola reached out for an eye.

"Well poised, Lola. Yes, indeed the eye is a center of symbolic translation and presentation from anywhere on the Planet of Great Consciousness. Although almost too much at times, for it can trigger ego weaknesses and narcissism. The eye does, as you say catalyze response, interpretation and even navigation. I see you have an eye in your hand. Is it sharing anything with you?"

Lola held the small globe in heshe's hand and sensed it's potential. Heshe began to see fire in the eye, then it changed to a scene of fighting, and finally it shifted to rainbows. "Whoa, maybe we can go to another filter, window or door? I am not sure this is how I want to enter the 3-D with this type of perspective, however, I may glean from it the idea of the empathic eye."

"Well then, remember, the difference between merely watching and the dynamic difference when one actually *sees*." Purpol snapped his fingers three times. "Of course, let's move on. Step back. Let's give it a whirl again!"

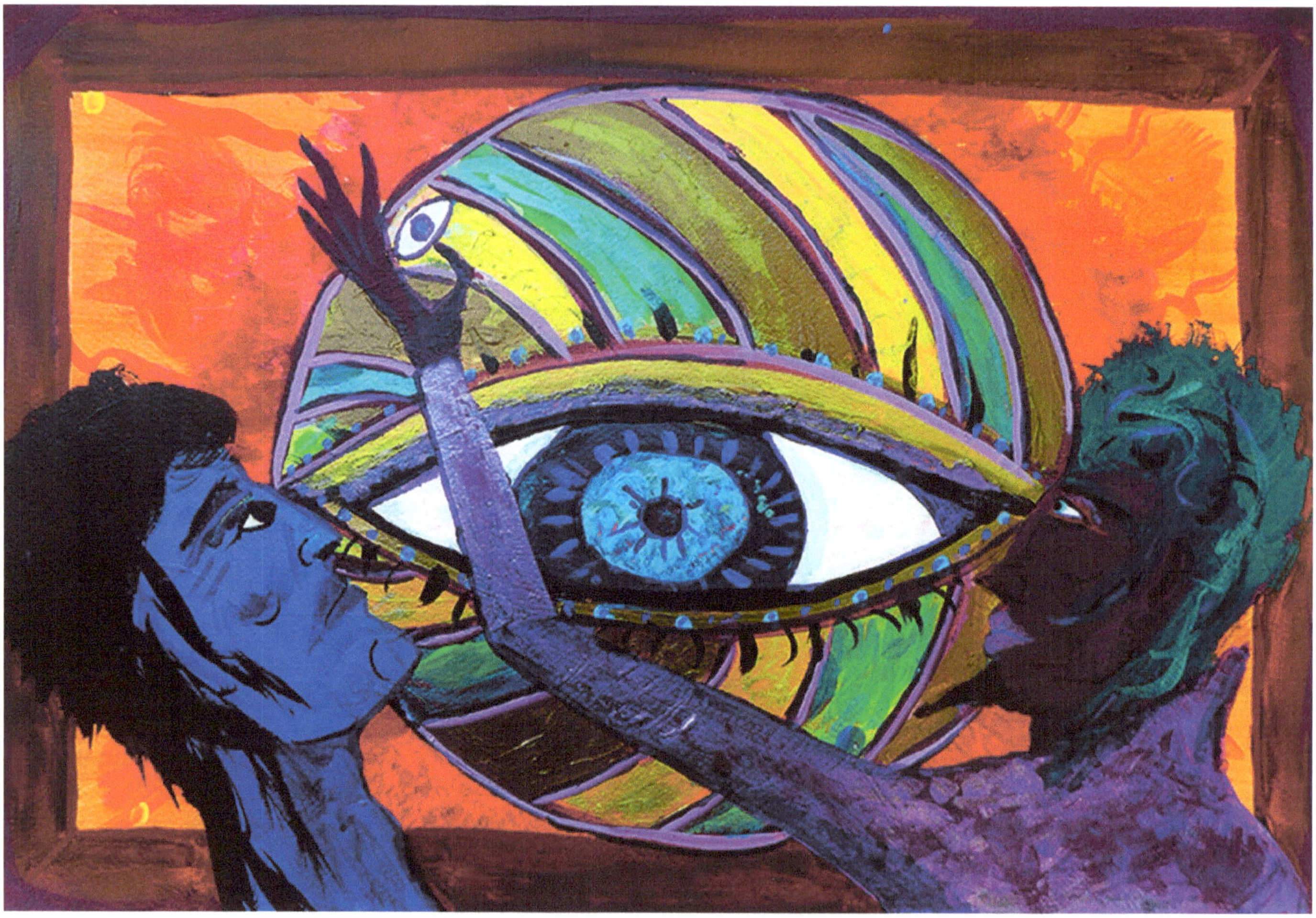

This window was much larger. In fact, it seemed larger than the house.

"These windows are about choice. Possibility. And now you see before you the filter of form and pattern. One could enter the realm of 3-D to be a pattern-tracker. That is, one who recognizes geometric formulas and interprets them. It's a way to navigate the world with a bit different emotional tone with more of reserved quality, perhaps even detached or ambivalent." Purpol raised his hand and waved it through the air and the window turned into several more windows. Windows within windows for as far as the eye could see.

The two stood dwarfed next to this portal of possibility.

"It looks like one pattern leads to another. But where do they lead?"

"The irony? They all lead back to themselves, the starting point or origin. Patterns within patterns…"

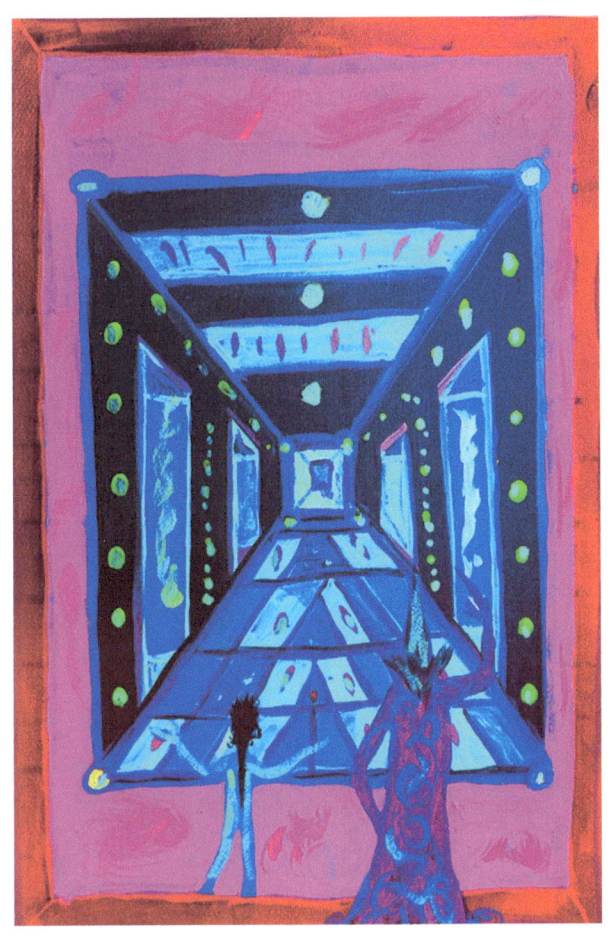

Lines, curves circles and squares!

Blend, merge, shape and form!

Awakening remembrance of the ALL

Diamonds, triangles and pyramids!

Illustrious mathematical pathways

Octahedron tetrahedron sri yantras

Sequences of magical movements

Miracles of visions remain untorn.

"*W*ell dear Lola, its nearly time to select your filter. I want you to open your mind and heart and ask for guidance. Which way, which view will guide you to your heart's desire." Purpol danced around the house, touching window after window and door after door, the house spun and spun. Then, Purpol snapped his fingers three times. "Let it be done. Let it be known! Which of you reveals the entry for dear Lola?"

In moments time a strange, warped door appeared. It was large, orange and yellow with bronze hinges. There was a tiny round window at the top. "Well, it seems you hit the jackpot! Two in one! A door **with** a window!"

The entryway had a large number seven painted on it. Purpol opened the door and out popped a wild looking clown. Dressed in head to toe with blue velvet and pink fringe, the dark faced jester spun around in the center of the room.

"Ah we have a seeker! A thinker. A searcher of truth! You have chosen lucky seven. My name is Siete de Portico de Sangria. Behind this very door are hidden truths, secret meanings, this filter helps you to remember to take nothing at face-value. There are many deceptions and delusions and control freakas on that planet! So it's wise of you to take that eye, the patterns, and me and let's all go together into the realm of 3-D pandemonium! Inside this place, you gonna see the 'T'. The truth… of course one man's truth is another man's house plant…or how does that limerick go? Well, never mind. Any last word little Lola?" The Klown paused. "Purpol, you got any blessings for this lad before they go down the magic hole?"

"Thank you Señor Siete. I'm ready as I'll ever be. And, thank you Purpol for leading me to this gate. I think it will serve me well." Lola reached for the knob.

"Wait! You must say the magical incantation three times and remember it by heart so you can come back here if need be."

All good children go heaven

When you open door number seven.

Seven gates of truth

Seven levels of wisdom

Seven portals of visions

Open and reveal

Open and reveal

Open and REVEAL!

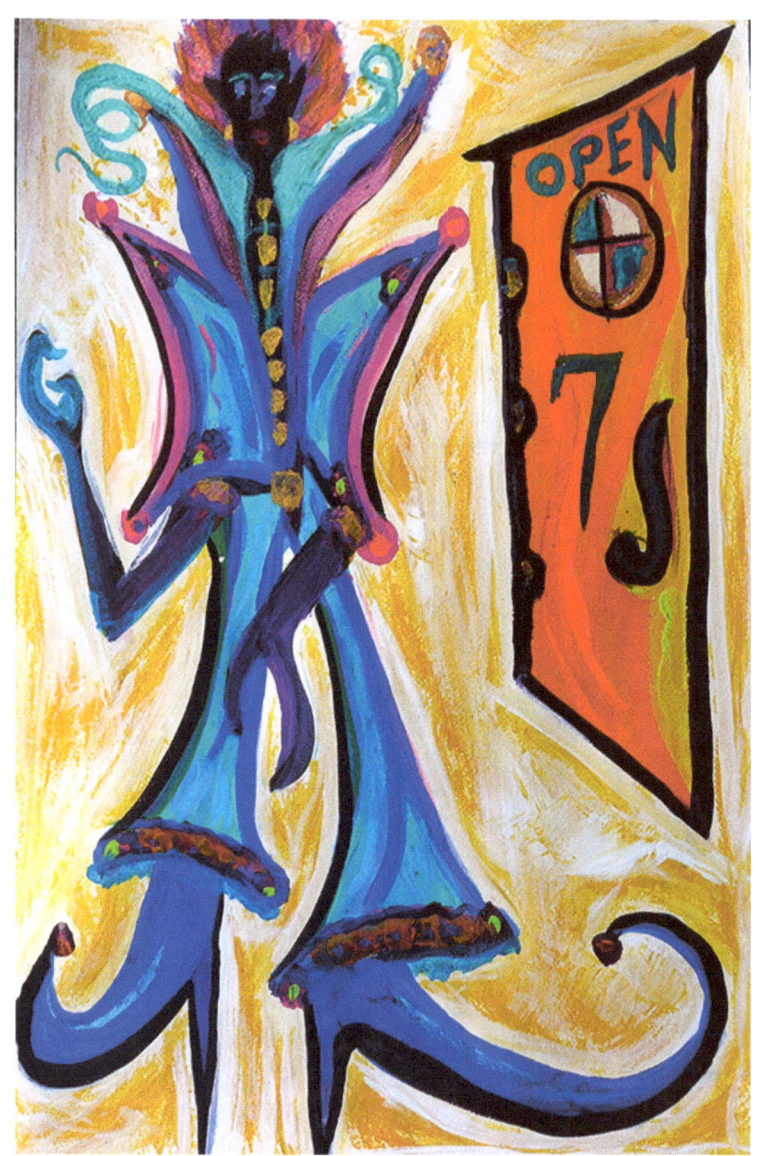

"*O*h yeah, show me THE WAY! This way and that way. Any way. Way OUT. So many books telling you the way to do it." Tricksta She-Low gazed upon a little blue lad approaching her. "Al right, I've got all the ways for you in this book. Wanna know which path? Which god? Which truth? Which witch? Bahahahahah!" She-Low shoved a book into the hands of a perplexed looking Lola.

"Er… he..he…Hello to you too! What's in this book? Do I need it?" Lola asked. All heshe could remember was walking through a door and poof Lola was on a dirt road. It looked like it led to a giant urban jungle off in the distance.

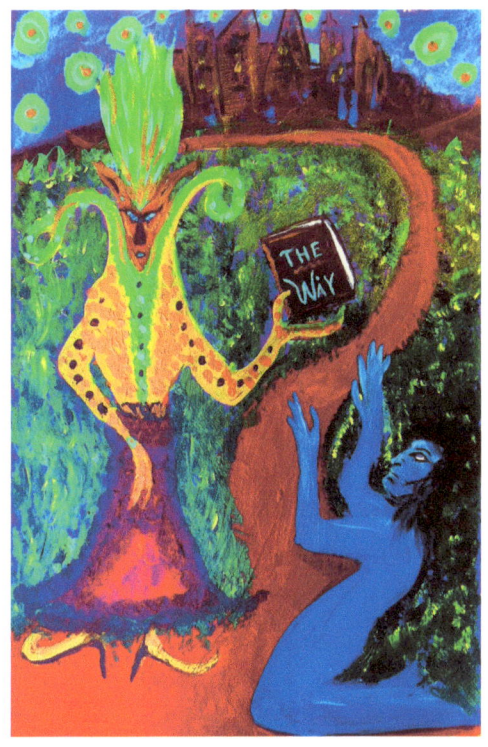

"Do. You. Need. It. Hmmm? Of course you need IT! Everyone wants THE BOOK, that shows them the way. Lots of curves, lots of paths. Lots of ways." She-Low bent over and gawked at Lola who now stooped before her. "You new around here or what?"

Lola took the book and glanced through it. It could be useful. Why not? "I'll take it. Thank you for the gift."

"Gift? Gurrrrrllll nothing free here! I gotta price. And you gotta pay for my advice."

"Ok how do I pay you then?" Lola asked.

"Hmmm… doesn't look like you got much on ya, so Ill settle for a story. Tell me about…your heart's desires! On second thought, nah, I don't really care. Take the book. Good luck. You'll need it. I'm outta here, I see my sister coming… uffff…good luck with that one! She a beeeeyatch" Tricksta stormed off in a puff of dust.

Lola looked down the road where a woman stood with green hair. She waved joyfully, motioning for heshe to join her.

"Hi there. Did my sister rattle your cage? I'm She-High." The lady looked the object in Lola's hands. "Oh dear, she gave you a copy of the Book of Ways, did she? Well you sure got a slap on the head with us two-facers…"

"Ah, She-Low didn't bother me. I guess I do need some guidance. I'm new here."

"Well, welcome to Dewalcitay. Two-sides of everything they say. Not sure who said that though." She-High pointed to the horizon.

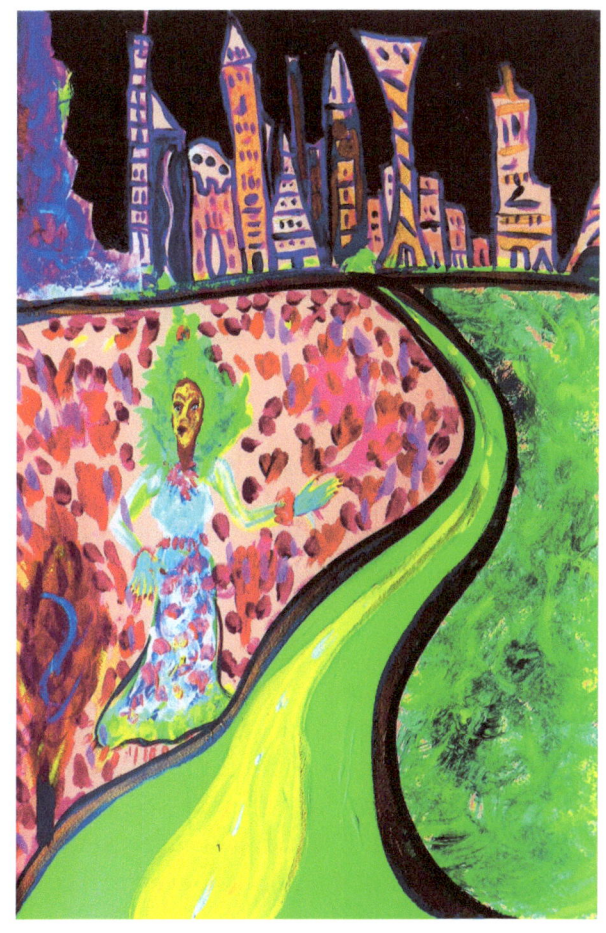

There it was, the urban jungle. But this time it no longer seemed so menacing, in fact, it looked delicious, pink, rose, amber, with sparkling lights. Lola stared at a large mountain in the distance behind the citay. "Where does this road go, beyond the citay? I'd love to meet new friends."

"Well this 'way' is the map that leads to the discovery of each individual's karma, their blueprint for conscious growth. There's a sheeeite full of hidden agendas in there so you better learn which side of the road you wanna be on."

13

Then all at once, one side of the road became a barren wasteland while the other remained green and lush. "Where does it lead you ask? Dreams. Into the night of dreams. If you're lucky, you'll make it to the Great Indigo Mountain the home of the Keepers of the Storybundles. But it's a hella long way. You gotta car?"

"A car? Um… no? I've got my feet." Lola giggled.

"Welp. Walk then it is. If you pass through the field, it's a short cut to the citay. And… a… stay outta trouble kid." She-High bowed to Lola and ran off into the barren landscape.

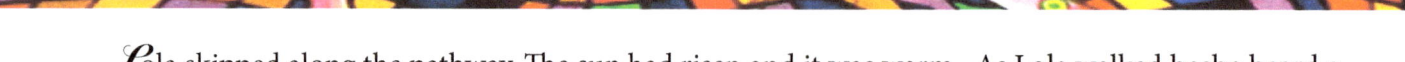

Lola skipped along the pathway. The sun had risen and it was warm. As Lola walked heshe heard a whimpering sound coming from a pile of debris. The stench was horrific. Lola furled their brow. "Do you need help? Is anyone in there?" Heshe poked at the pile of stuff. Tin cans, plastic wrappers of every sort were strewn across a large portion of the field.

"I'm not 'in' here. I'm all of this! I'm known in these parts as 'Dragg Trasher'. I'm kinda sad, they haven't fed me today… all this recycling n baloney… I gotta wait for waste around these parts for my fill. It's not

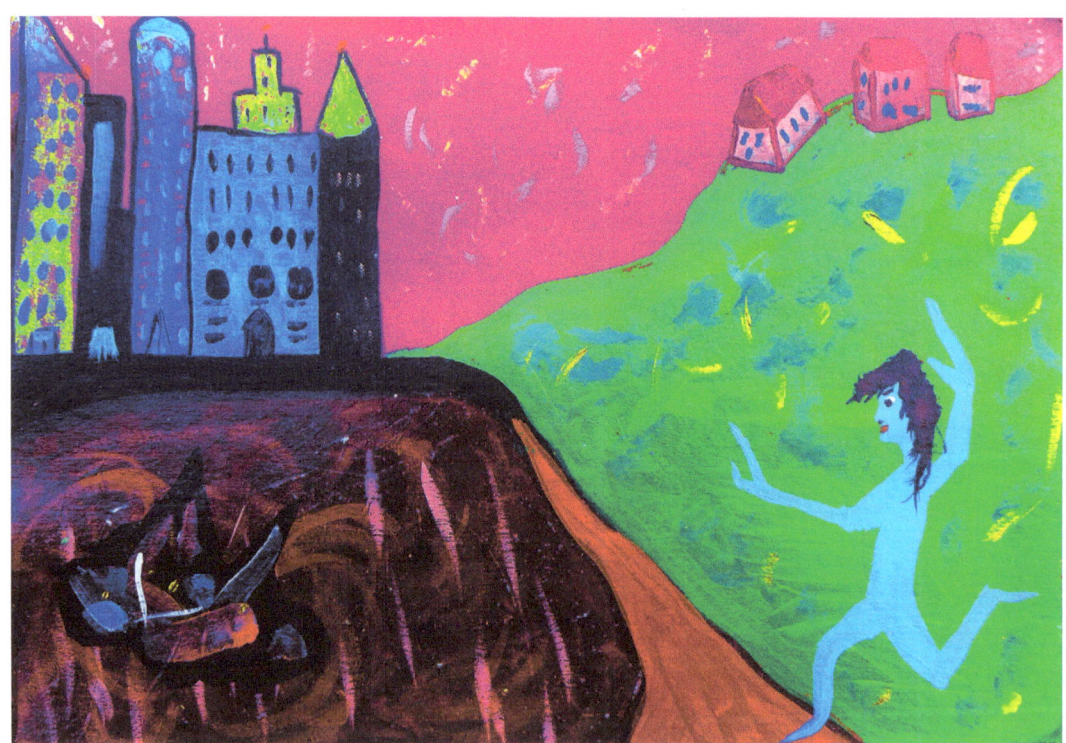

like that in my cousin's neighborhood. She's closer to all the poh' people. They gotta a whole lotta plastic crap to throw out."

"What do you mean throw out? I'm sorry, but I'm not from around here." Lola wanted to pinch heshe's nose from the horrific stench, but then decided it may be rude. Think empathic eye… remembered Lola.

"Oh boy, you are lame gurl. See those homes over there? Thas suburpia. It's the homes of the Toss Aways. Well, this is masssssss consumpshun junkshun. This is where the buck stops. Or is it the truck? Anyway, everything is packaged, processed, bought, sold and tossed my way. To rot. The seagullas love me though. But to tell you the truth, I'm sick of it. In the old days these piles … my cousins, the Trasshers… well, there wasn't all this plastic around. It even makes someone like me sick to my stomach."

"Why do they do it if it's not good for them," asked Lola?

"Dunno. Lazy. Patterns. Been doing it awhile. Don't wanna let go? Who knows, but they gonna kill this planeta! Das fo sho." Dragg Trasher picked up a plastic gun, it had been cracked and it's handle hung swinging in the air. "Ratt tatta tat atatt. They rather spend time fightin' for more and more and more and more and more! The law of MORE!"

"Wow. Well I'm gonna help them do something about that," exclaimed Lola!

"You do that. You go do that… there's the path to the source of it all. Dewalcitay. Well anyway, I'm goin' back to my cave. Have a good one…"

*W*ell, I'm on a journey, that's for sure. Lola continued down the road and entered the Dewalcitay. This time heshe was excited, a bit amused by the quirkiness of it all. The lights. The sounds. But one thing heshe wasn't ready for were the homolessnessers. Lola strolled upon the sidewalks and saw one after another of the humanos laying on a cardboard box on the ground. Heshe's heart became heavy. How was this so? I wonder if there is anyone to discuss this in the citay? Lola found a small green area with a tree and some flowers and sat down. Soon afterward, heshe was joined by an astonishingly tall humano, dressed head to toe in worn, black denim.

"Hiya kid, new to the citay? I'm Bleek. I live up there on the roof of that building. Boy what a view! Wanna come up and see it?" Bleek pointed to the roof of a multi-story building on the next street.

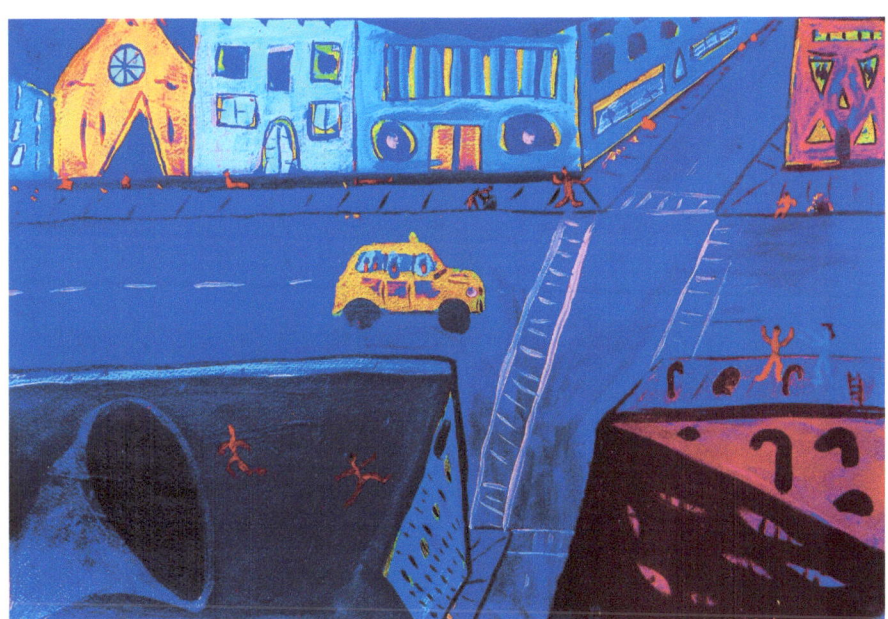

"Why not? I'm Lola. But pardon me, I don't get all the humanos just sleeping on the ground here, isn't it cold?" Lola stood up and followed Bleek to an old wooden door.

"Come on up here. Ill share a little 'bout my take of this sitchuwayshun."

They climbed stair after stair, it seemed endless until at last Lola felt a draft of fresh air. "WOW! What a view. This is so cool. You live up here?"

Bleek pulled out a large cart with several bags hanging from the sides. "Yup this is my room with a view. Amazin. Ain't it? In a world of so much and we ain't got nuttin. I used to have a house. But a big ole' bankeroo came and took it all away. They want more and more and more to cover their costs, so they say. So, I ended up here. I feel lucky, cuz those down there, they only have a doorway to sleep in."

Lola had no words. Heshe just sat for awhile taking it all in. Some of it had felt exciting about the citay, but this was excruciatingly sad. Lola watched Bleek fall asleep next to a large steel pipe. Then, Lola heard a soft murmur.

Just a stone's throw
And you can get a blow
Knocked down by poverTea
It's not always as you see.
Ticks n stones.
Bricks n bones.
Down to the skinny skin
Of nothin' left but what's within.

𝒯he next day, Bleek sent Lola to a rest-a-RANT to satisfy heshe's hunger to know. Once inside, Lola felt a startling emptiness. The place was stark and smelled of chemicals. There were no humanos inside though there were strange noises coming from behind a large silver door.

Lola was hungry. Heshe looked at the wall above a shiny metal counter. A bulletin board had large numbers printed that read '*2 for 1*'. Hmm? Lola walked over to the counter and saw colorful dishes and steaming foods. However, Lola didn't recognize any of them except for the fruits. A sullen, grey faced humano approached the counter and asked Lola what heshe wanted to eat.

"I'd like to try a little bit of everything. Thank you. I'm not able to identify any of these foods. Are they what everyone eats here," asked Lola?

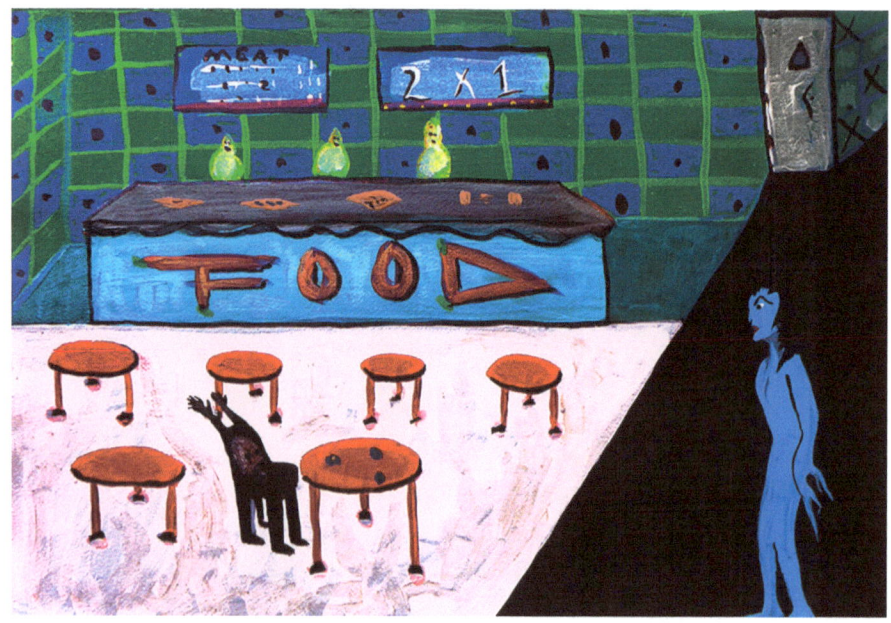

"Everyone eats whatever they can afford to pay, I guess. And I suppose if they don't eat meat, or are allergic, or addicted… or…" The humano continued to rant about the food while Lola heard a soft whistling sound coming from the dining area.

"Pssst…pssst…Lola! Over here", whispered a chair.

Lola wasn't that surprised when the chair spoke since heshe had also just heard the lament of the stones which formed the building where Bleek lived. Lola answered, "Um… hi?"

"I'm Chair Itea. Listen. I've got some change for you. Come over here and sit at my table. Get whatever you want." The chair wobbled and some coins fell on the floor. Lola picked them up and walked to the counter and purchased some colorful items to eat.

"Thank you. I'm Lola. I've never had to buy food before. What am I eating?"

"Wow, you must be from the other realms. Especially if you can hear me. You are eating crap. Complete processed, dead food. Although, those fruits look OK. Have you ever been to a rest-a-RANT," asked the chair?

"Never," paused Lola. "Why did you say this is dead food? It looks so colorful and kinda yummy."

"It's been in the freezer for 2 weeks. On the counter for 3 days. And was in a warehouse for 1 month. On a truck for 2 weeks. And in another warehouse for 1 week after it was picked green mind you—not ripe! So in my wonky opine, it's dead food. 2 months to your stomach… bleeeeeeck!." Chair Itea leaned back on 2 legs.

"Wow, in the past, I've pretty much just picked things from plants wherever I walked when I lived in the selva."

"This is what you deal with here. Humanos are super desensitized from poisoned food. Sound pollution. And lack of compassionate touch. They are sensory numbed. Ah well… there I go ranting again… but it is a rest-a-RANT, ya know?"

"Wow. I've never thought about that perspective of humanos. But it makes sense. So many seem like zombias. Well, now I have a better idea of what to contend with while I'm here. Thank you! Any ideas on where I should go next to learn about the plight of humanos," Lola asked the chair?

"Hmmmm. Well, why not go to a food factory. Then you'll see what I'm talking about."

"Thanks, I'll do that."

---

*L*ola set out with directions from Chair Itea. Heshe approached an enormous grey building had been described by the chair. A large sign read, 'STUFF CO.' There were strange whirring and thunking sounds coming from behind the walls. Thousands of vehiculos were stationed on a large black sheet of tar. There were no trees to ask questions. There were some strips of grass, perhaps heshe could summon them to share news. Just then, a furry, aged ratita scurried towards Lola.

"Hey. Hey. I've been expecting you. Word has it you're here to help us? Oh. My. My. Come over here where we can chat and not get noticed." The ratita seemed a little nervous.

"Cool. Thanks. Yes, Chair Itea sent me to discover how food is…um… processed?"

"This is a confunction confection fabrica. Look in the windows. See those straps and flaps, wheels n cogs, and those puffs and spurts? That's corn and wheat and sugar and goo mashed together to create what humanos call a SeeReeal. They're addicted to them. Over there? That's the office of the execusticks who run the operation. They control all the twerkers who labor here."

"Whoa…. Slow down a minute. This is food? Where are all the plants you spoke of, like the corn," asked Lola?

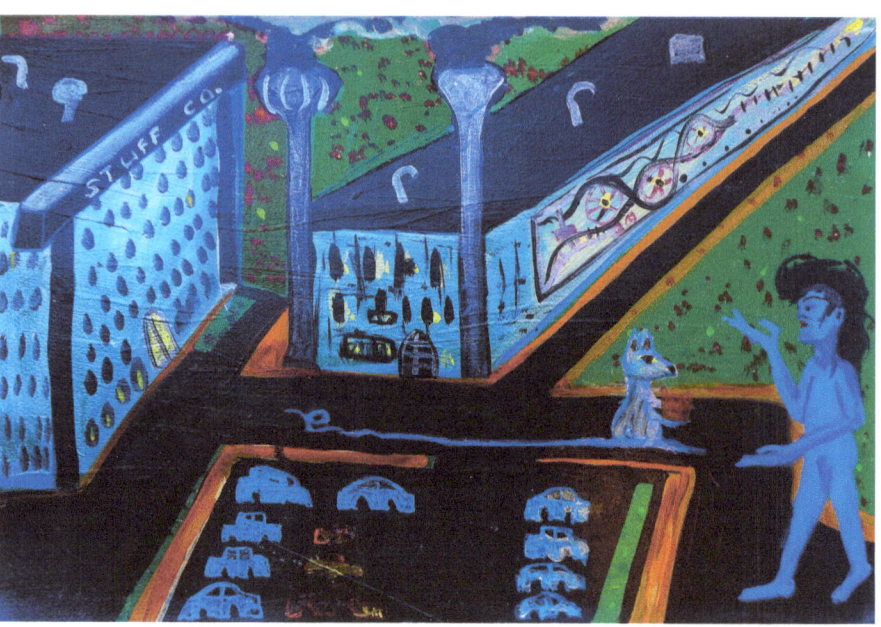

"Thousands of miles from here. Brought in by train. They put this stuff in colorful boxes with funny lookin' animals on the covers. Strange. They never want to put me on the cover." Ratita sighed. "Ah well. I see they put lots of cats on things…not fair."

"But you speak of addiction? Why?"

"Chemicals. They put in zybuplovin, zapmorplaca, zombiadoo and stuff that numb the humanos brains. They call em G-MOES. Alterin' the DNA. That's crazy shit man. Gets em depressed so they don't wanna do nothing 'cept sit in front of a zombie box." Ratita scuttled to some grass and began to gnaw on the greens.

"Zombie box? You sure are giving me a lot to chew on… jejeje…," giggled Lola.

"Funny. Sure. Ok. You really aren't from this dimensia…I mean dimension. Ok. A zombie box transmits images through the air. It controls their minds too. You're gonna find out that there's a whole lotta things controlling humanos minds. Hope you got ideas on how to help em? Anyway, I gotta run." Ratita glanced back for a second. "Go check out the Candee shop. Taste something there and you'll figure this addiction out… when you try some shooogar! My friend runs the shop, YUM. You'll love her."

*I*t was absolutely the most flamboyant place Lola had seen yet in the 3-D realm. Dazzling colors, shapes, smells. It was unbearable. Lola looked around for heshe's host, YUM.

"Hello? Hello? YUM? I'm Lola, Ratita sent me. This place is astonishing!" Lola waited for someone to come into the room. Then, a huge rumble and a machine in the center of the room began to speak.

"OF COURSE IT'S ASTONISHING! WELCOME TO THE SHOOGAR MILL. I AM YUM. QUEEN OF SWEETNESS." She shouted and candees fell from her mouth as she spoke.

"Did you make all this? These sweet things," asked Lola?

Before heshe could say anything else, tiny Brownies darted around the room collecting the candees that had fallen from YUM. They began to devour them. Then they began to eat the wall, the floor, the posts, everything it seemed was sweet and edible. "JOIN US," shouted the Brownies!

They seem a bit crazed, thought Lola. "Um… OK!" Lola reached out to what appeared like a tree and grabbed a LolyPop! Heshe began to chew and lick on it. In a few moments heshe's glee turned to melancholy.

Lola's stomach began to rumble and heshe's tongue tasted like metal. This was shooogar?

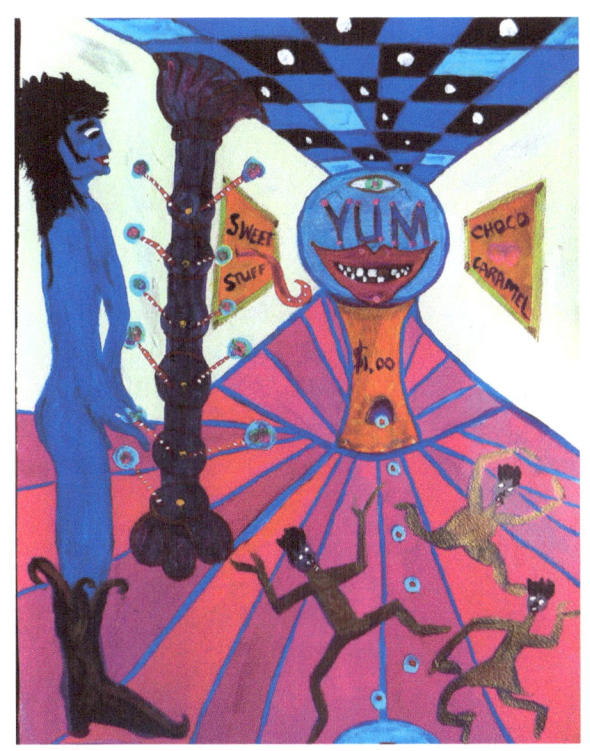

"YOU LIKE IT? OF COURSE YOU DO? I'VE GOT CHOCO LATTES. GOODROPS. CREEEMEEE PUUFFS. BONNY BONS. YOU NAME IT AND I CAN CONFECT IT. SHOOOOOOOOGAR IS MY GAME! QUEEN OF SWEETNESS I AM!" YUM smiled revealing blackened teeth and a few were covered in gold. Her breath stank.

"Hey, thanks YUM. Interesting stuff you make here, but I don't think its for me. I gotta run!" Lola scurried out the door.

YUM shouted threats at Lola. "YOU IDIOT. YOU LOVE SHOOGAR! COME BAAAAAACK HERE. I WANT YOU TO GET HIGH ON MY SWEETNESS!"

*W*hile, Lola was a little shaken, heshe was ready to take on the quirkiness of the 3-D realm. Surely, there must be places where humanos who were evolving visited? Or was everyone hooked and befouled by bad foods? Lola strolled the evening streets. In the distance heshe saw a giant glowing tongue in front of a building. It reminded heshe of the Carnival. Well perhaps there was hope inside this place?

Lola opened the doors to the Golden Tongue establishment. Heshe relaxed a bit. Inside was the soothing smell of frankinsensia incense and the sounds of comforting music. The seats were plush and the humanos seemed relaxed and enjoying themselves. Lola sat at a table. An ornately dressed elder gentleman approached Lola's table with a smile. "Greetings Lola. I am Grass Hoppre. You look like you could use a break? Let me share with you about this marvelous place. The Golden Tongue."

"Thank you, yes. I've just spent time in a rest-a-RANT, with the homelessness, at the ShoogarMill and a Seee Reeeal factory. It's been a bit unnerving to witness such incongruent manner in the 3-D realms. Yet, you seem to assure me that there are some magical parts?" Lola sat back in the plush red velvet couch.

"In here is a magical theatre. Upstairs you can have your fortune told. And over there we have a knick-knack shop. It sounds like your journey has revealed the trickery in the seduction of humanos. However, there are many who are well on their way to join you in 5-D one day. Often, it seems, that humanos take for-granted that everything they do is a form of magic? Speaking. Thinking. Even eating!"

"Where can I go to meet more of these people? Is there anywhere out of the citay for a bit? I would like to rest under some trees and contemplate what I've experienced so far," inquired Lola.

"Why yes, there is. And perfect timing! The next few days is what is referred to as a crossing quarters event. I'll send you to a place in a meadow with the RadFaes. A whimsical, non-traditional or extremely indescribable group. But, they are certainly entertaining and ready to share deeper thoughts about the Planet of Great Consciousness. Here is the address of my friend Dev Lish. In the meantime, take in the sights of this enchanting place." Grass Hoppre stood up and motioned for someone to bring Lola a cup of tea.

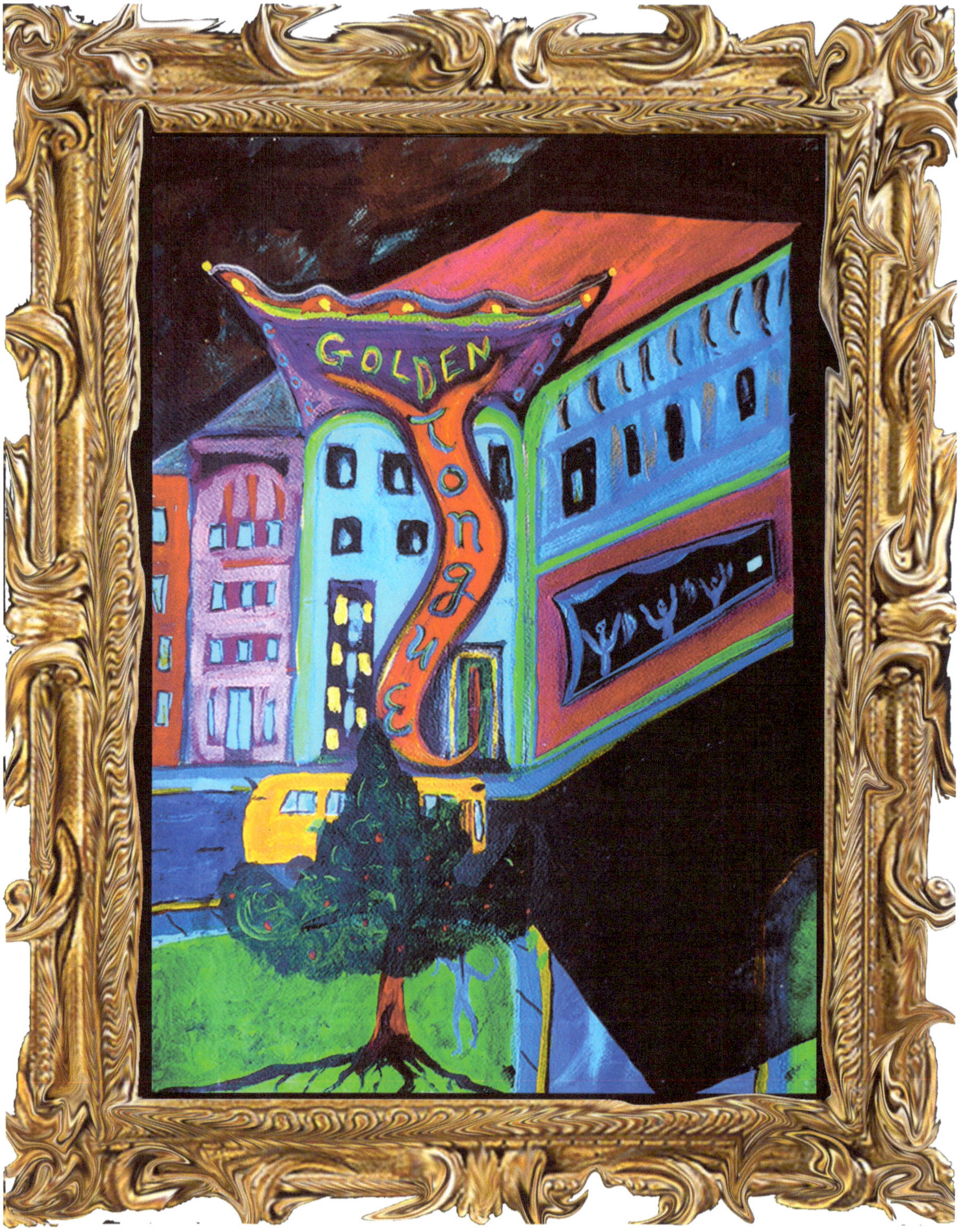

$\mathcal{T}$he night was chilly and Lola longed for the warmth of the selva. Lola had seen some very strange beings out tonight. Many of them looked terrifying. Monstros, Goulies and ghosters. Heshe hesitated in front of the sizeable, indigo house. It had three gabled windows on the second story. Lola gazed up at the sky. To heshe's delight, there she was, Luna Blanca!

"Luna! Wow! You surprised me! What do you know about this place? I was told there were interesting humanos at this house? Any ideas? I also observed a few very strange creatures out tonight."

"Ah. Lola, it is all hallows eve. Many of the humanos wear costumes to celebrate. Although it's just a party now, it used to remind those to honor the eight gates for Gaia passage around dear Sol. Yes Lola, I do believe there are those in this house who will reveal a bit more depth to your exploration of the humanos and their 3-D experience." Luna winked at Lola and continued to rise up into the sky.

Lola knocked on the door. There was laughter coming from inside and strange blinking lights flashed.

"Tricks or Treats which shall it be!" The door opened quickly and a startling green woman with a pointy hat. She held an orange, pumpkin-shaped basket in her hand.

"I was sent here by Grass Hoppre from the Golden Tongue?" Lola then added, "What is a trick or treat?" Heshe stepped into the house where two other beings sat smiling on a green couch.

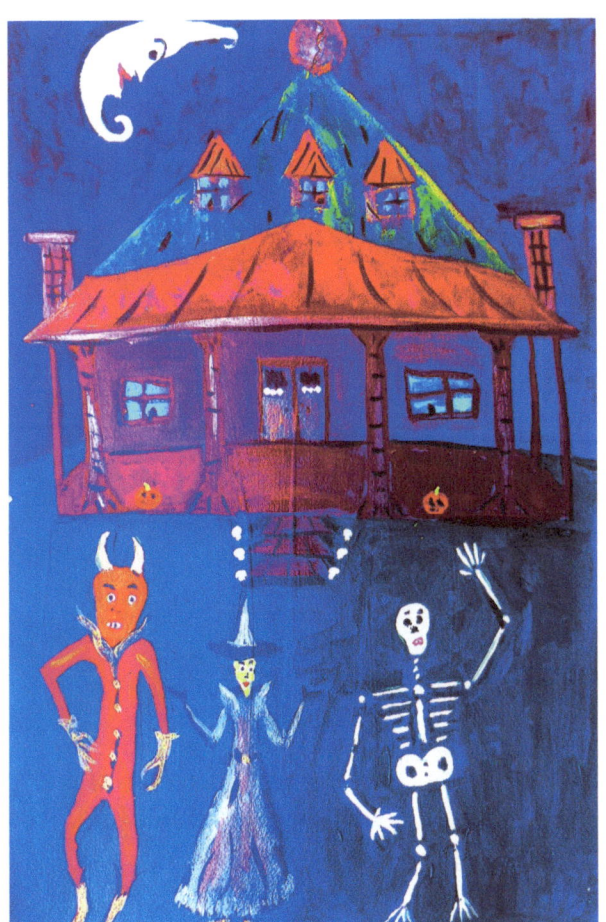

"Oooooo. Where are you from? Grass Hoppre? Well then, you are most welcome! Tricks are for kids. Treats are for witches. Bahahahaha. Nah, I'm just joking. Haven't you experience Halloweenie? It's really amateur day if you ask me…" Witcheela put down the basket and twirled about in the room.

"Hey kid, I'm Dev Lish and this is Boner. We're going to take a walk around the gayborhood. Wanna join us?"

"Ah yes, Dev Lish, Grass Hoppre mentioned you. Sure. Let's take a walk, but I need something warmer to put on my body. Why are there so many strange looking humanos out there tonight with baskets," asked Lola?

"Halloweenie is the time when the normalies get to do what we do anytime we want! Celebrate the body with costumes and adornments. They dress in caricatures of their Holy Wood icons. And some of us just get weird and emphasize characteristics of ourselves. Like Witcheela is a real witch. Some may call me the Deveeel, but I just like to make folks laugh at their troubles. And Boner, here, well, you get the point."

"Ah come on, Dev Lish, it's also a time to honor the ancestors. Ya know, those that came before us?" Witcheeela picked up a fotograph of a grey haired woman. "This was my grammy. She was a lovely witch. All hail to the ancestrsos!"

"Hey Lola, tomorrow you should join us and drive out to the sanctuario and meet some of the other RadFae. If you like it, we can show you how we create ceremonias."

"It feels like you are the jaguar magicians I've been looking for, the double-spirited beings or …qwa qwa qwurs." Lola picked up an apple from the table, "May I?"

"Yes, of course, and we are Queers. Odd, Mysterious. Unusual. Some of the gang may be the jaguar magicians you speak of. There's a lot of variety in our tribe."

Dev Lish, Boner, Witcheeela and Lola proceeded to go out and 'trick o treat'.

Lola arrived at the sanctuario of the RadFae and spent a few months while heshe enjoyed learning about ritual and intentions in the qweer commune. Heshe attended circulos del Corazon, where emotions were revealed and unraveled. Lola became quite fond of this group. Then one day they announced it was time to hold the Bell Taint ceremonia.

"Hey Dev Lish, can you share more about this endeavor? I mean the pole is beautiful, but why do you do this?" Lola wanted to know everything heshe could.

"The pole is a giant male member and the hole is the female member and together they get married and we all live happily ever after," laughed Dev Lish.

"NOT. Well sorta." Witcheeela grabbed Lola's hand and brought heshe to the meadow where the celebration was beginning. "Sometimes, our ancestors shared that there were ways to mirror gratitude for the divine mystery. This is the time of year when so many things begin to flower, sprout and seed. It's a time of growth after a long incubation. We dance around it weaving our prayers. It's symbolic of course, yet, by doing so with our will focused, it generates energy for manifesting our dreams. And some say it's a day to wed oneself to their heart's desires. What's your heart desire, Lola?"

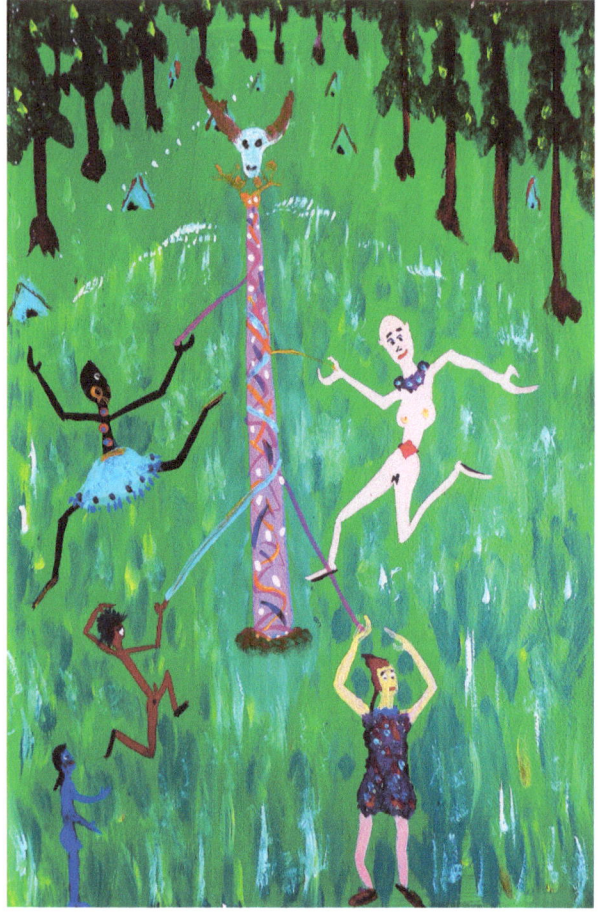

Lola thought for a bit, heshe knew that magic was real and didn't want to overstep with an unfocused intention. Then at once heshe knew. "Honestly, I would like to continue to grow to understand humanos and help guide them, or mirror for them, ways to release fear, to celebrate the mystery and to drop the hating and get on with the love. If my heart felt this, I would be so happy for all of us. May I wrap that into the post?" Lola grabbed a ribbon and joined the others.

Later that evening, Lola felt it was time to let them know that heshe was going to move on and explore other dynamic parts of Gaia. That night there had been a theatre amongst the friends. Lola had met a wonderful mask-a-tier named Marvavilla. Lola's new friend had invited Lola to learn about how humanos are able to travel to other realit-teas.

Marvavilla stepped out onto stage that night carrying spider marionnettas. The mask-a-tier pranced about on stage and spoke about weaving community and webs of creation. Lola thought back to the time heshe spent with Zuvuyana. While Lola was in 3-D what could heshe weave? Harmony? Ideas? Directions? The more time heshe spent in 3-D it became clear how complex the Gaiaic realm of duality was and why it had become perilously close to destruction.

"Hey Marvavilla what do you think theatre is? I mean, you get up there and you perform. Isn't the life of a humano a big performance of masks, I mean when it comes down to identity," asked Lola?

"Good point. I think on stage, at least for me, it's a time to bring attention to something. Perhaps even to transform it on stage. For example, I take the seemingly insignificance of a spider and turn its story into a magical being…especially to those who only see them as pests. I think it's important to help others contemplate that they are in a giant playhouse of their soul's evolution, and it's essential to take responsibility for their theatric messages? War? Lust for more? Disease? It's more than positive thinking, perhaps it's to help the viewers to see themselves as directors of the show rather than just the audience or victim." Marvavilla danced around on stage and sang a song,

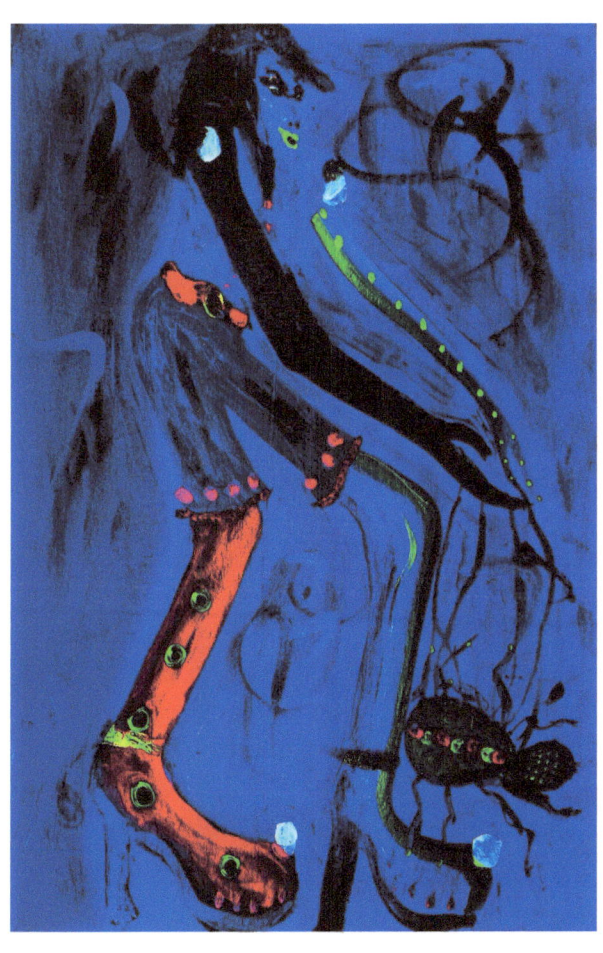

Everything's for sale!
Even the whales!
The seduction of false prophets
Won't take their hands off it!
I want this! I want that!
Puppets on a string
Your neck's in a ring!
Puppets profits!
Snip! Snip! Snip!
Cut the ropes!
But don't lose hope!

Marvavilla stepped down off the stage and took Lola's hand. "Hey Lola have you ever gotten to know the 'fun-guys'?"

"Hm… I think so. I was having this time with Gaia and Star Nunki. I was having a challenging time and Gaia gave me a special elixira. It opened me up to the Rains of Inspiration and it began to shower all kinds of shroomies. 'Fun-guys' as you call them? I do remember I felt great!"

"Well let's go take some if you like… and see who we meet to help you on your journey here. It can't be easy for you. Even though you are from another dimension, we all have that in us, you just remember more. Gosh, I hope we can be good friends."

Marvavilla and Lola went into the forest and drank some magical elixira and waited for messengers to come.

Within moments, Lola felt the sensation of being moved forward very quickly, even though heshe was sitting next to Marvavilla. Lola heard someone singing in the distance. Heshe saw what looked like a lit match coming towards both of them crawling across the floor. The light got brighter and brighter until it formed into a bizarre feminina. Her hair was brilliant orange and she had light blue skin. She was doing contortionist movements, like the one's heshe had seen in the Circo de Duendes.

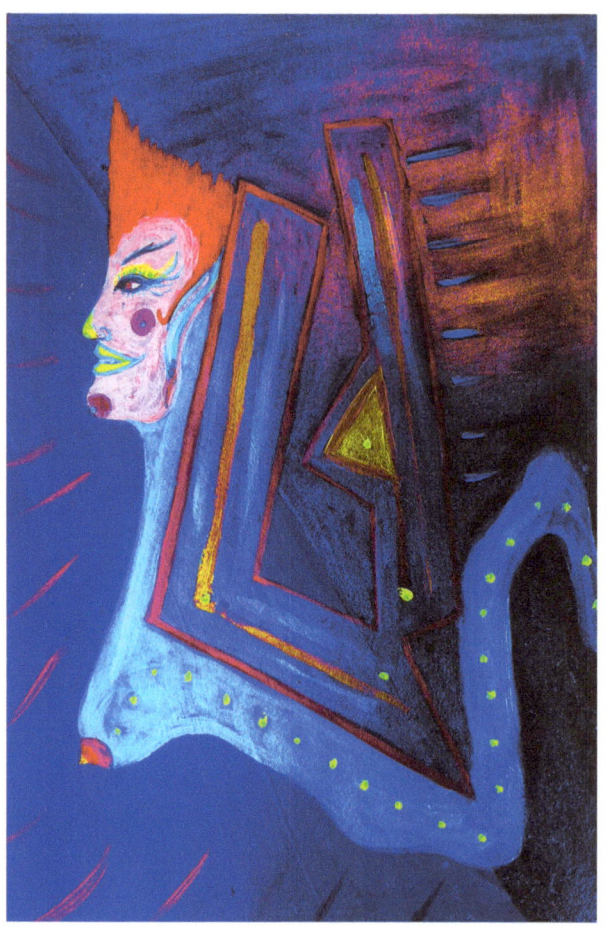

"Lalalalalalala Lolalalalalalalala LOlalaalalala. I'm the Fractal Chick boiz. Nice to see ya'll. How you doing there Lola? 3-D sucks. Well, unless you like cake. LET THEM EAT CAKE. Have your cake and eat it two!... Lalalalalala lalalalalla lalalalal Lola. Whatcha doing out here in the quantum fisica aspects? Getting curiouser? Wonderin' wanderer."

Lola was bedazzled. Heshe had visited these coordinates of the mind on journeys, but humanos could do it too? Wow. "Well this gives me hope. Fractal Chick…you remind me of an old friend, Payaso Pyneal."

Fractal Chick had more of a geometric shape than an actual body. It kept changing like a collide-a-scope. "Oh yeah. I know that dude. He's friggin awesome. Welp. This is what humanos can reach. Ya know the activation station of the 3-d to the 4-d to the 5-d and on and on… take a little trip… take a little trip inside me!"

Meanwhile, it seemed Marvavilla was conversing with someone else. Lola tried to reach out and touch Fractal Chick to see if she was real.

"Boundaries there, dude," shouted Fracktal! She smiled. "So, do me a favor. Help them humanos to remember that their ideas and intentions… every dang thought creates energy to form into a real-it-tea. The imagery is real, yeah for sure, but its also unreal. Mind over matter. Ya know? Hey you better go help your friend… he's on another plateau, buh bye wizard!" Fractal sparked into a million pieces and vanished.

Lola walked over to see why Marvavilla was so amazed. Heshe's friend sat in front of a huge clock. Boner had come to join them.

"hehehehe… Lola. I saw the Fractal Chick and you talking and I stood up and walked over here and met Boner. Isn't this clock cool? What do you think it's trying to tell us? It only has 1, 2 and 3 o'clock on it. Hehehehehe." Marvavilla reached out to turn the hands on the clock when out of it's internal chamber jumped a tiny man.

"Don't touch those hands without my permission. I control time!"

"Well ok, so who are you little guy? Heheehe", asked Marvavilla.

The little man swayed from the pendulum while whistling a haunting tune.

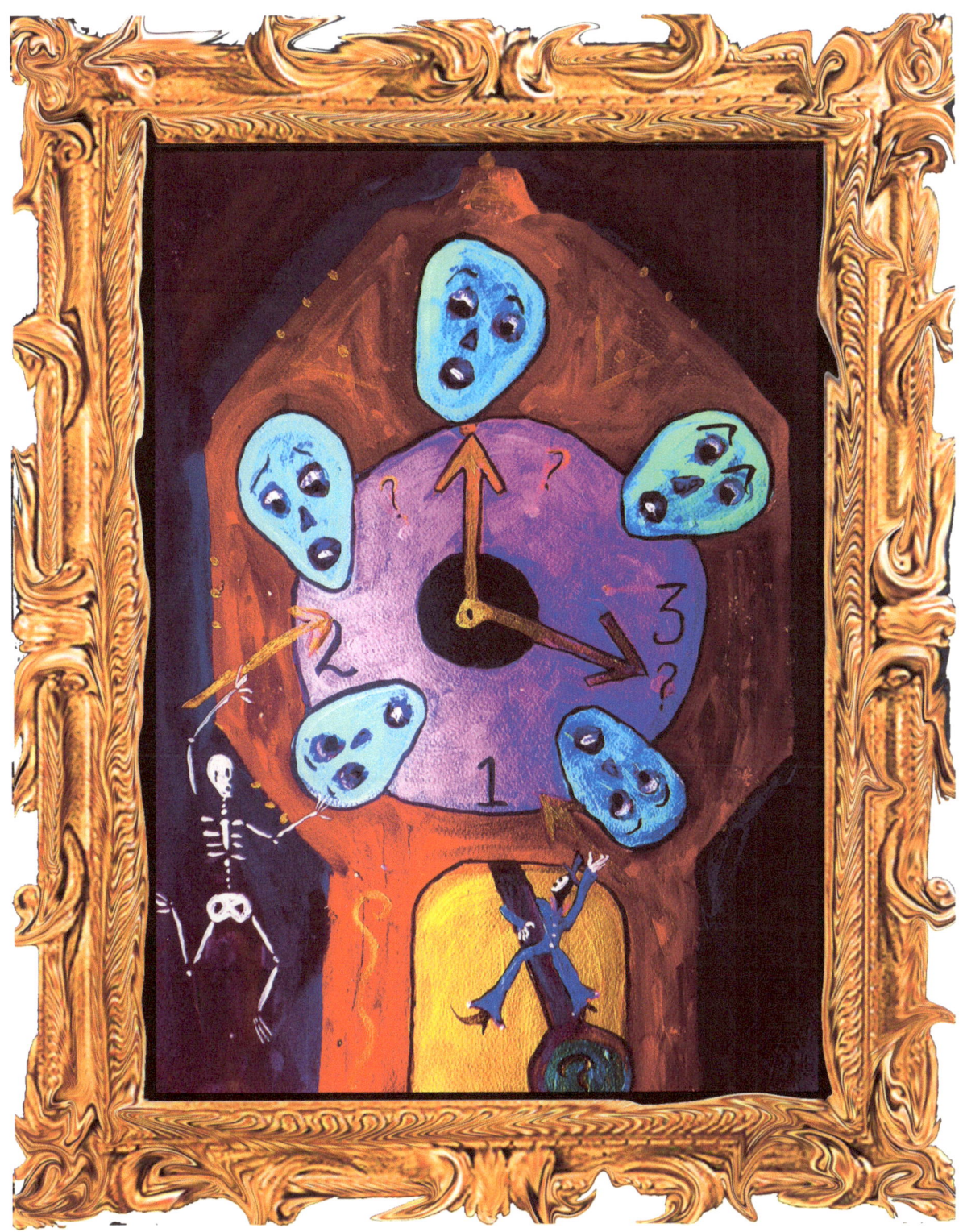

Does anyone know what time it si?
Tick. Tock. I am a clock!
Pick. Pock. Go take a walk.
I've got all the time in the world.
And for you I'll give it a twirl.
3 o'clock. 4 o'clock.
10 o'clock is the deadline.
For the sublime.

"Mr. Minutes why are you and Boner throwing arrows at the clock," laughed Lola?

"We are piercing time. Fast forward. Rewind. No one is ever late, we just keep moving the arms of the clock to make it convenient for anyone. Time is an illusion anyway. We are the masters of time-bending. I'll show you how I swing back and forth from time to time, carrying with me the past as if it's the future, the future as if it's now… well you'll get it. Tralalalalala."

Lola and Marvavilla sat and watched as Mr. Minutes and Boner. They seemed to compete for what time was showing on the clock. They tossed so many arrows at once, no one could see where the arrows landed. Meanwhile, Lola felt sleepy and curled up next to Marvavilla and started to dream.

Lola dreamt that heshe was in a strange, bluish-white room. There was a lovely woman dressed in rose and violet chiffon who approached Lola holding a large mirror. A small green man reached out to Lola and offered heshe a purple and gold cube. At the same time, Lola felt a strange sensation that something was behind and turned to see another head had popped out of their shoulder!

"Lola you are in the room of reflecshun with your divine twin, your twin flame, Morgano. I am Reflectiva and this is my helper the Emulator. Together we have some medicine for you while your mind is so open…especially since you are in the 3-D realms."

"Mmmm…mmm Morgano? How did you get here? Where's Marvavilla?"

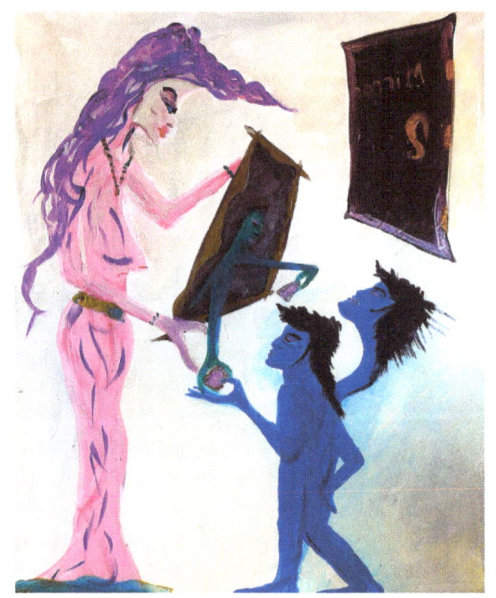

"Lola, I am always with you, remember? Perhaps, I am Marvavilla. Well in any case, we'll give you some clues to help the humanos and yourself so you don't get stuck in the reflections of 3-D. Be mindful of not getting too attached to anything you see. The challenges that you'll face will also change you just by being there for a time. Remember that. Humanos have come to agreements for themselves on their soul pathways to 5-D. You carry such a high vibration, it's likely wherever you go, anyone can feel it. Yet, be aware there are sinistros and that for some reason want to keep humanos as slaves and control them… thus to prevent them from evolving—which also may ultimately help them to destroy their planeta! It's happened before in the universe. But, don't fret. Ride it as easy as you can. Breaking attachments is as easy as shifting your mind. Teach them the practice of mind-fullness."

Reflectiva pulled the mirror back and the little green man disappeared. "The cube is a key. It will open the door behind you and reverse the reality to take you back to 3-D. Go on, Lola."

Lola turned around, Morgano had disappeared as well. Heshe took the advice and placed the cube in a slot on the door suddenly found themselves in a barnyard.

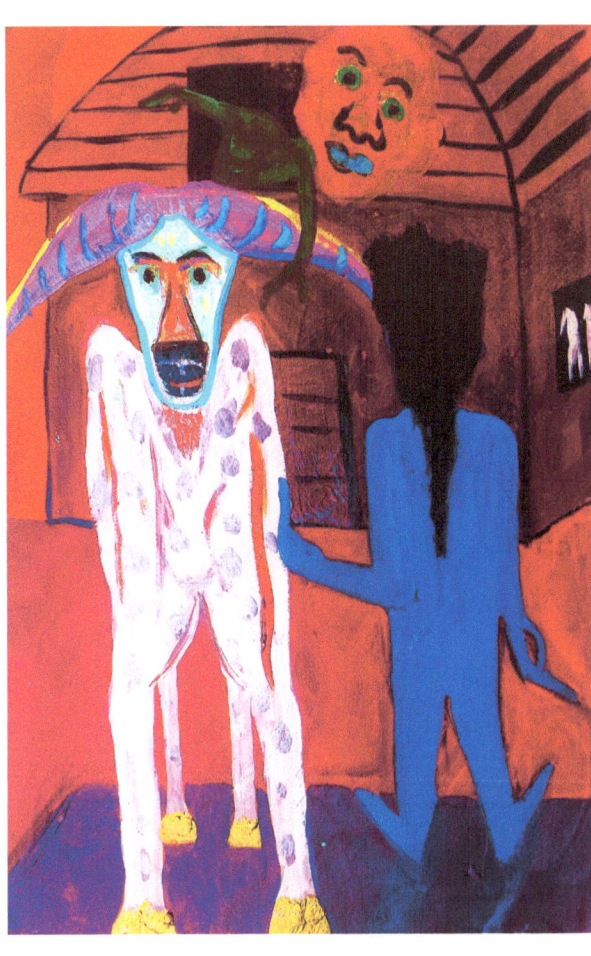

𝓛ola woke and spat hay from their mouth. Heshe heard a vacacow moo.

"Wake up dear one. It's time for milking. I'm Lecche de Vackita. You've had a long night. Your friend, Marvavilla brought you here to keep you warm and have a good rest. He said he would run into you later… at the theatre."

"Oh. Wow. OK." Lola still felt the effects from the elixira. Heshe walked outside with Lecche. "Oooo… how strange! Why is everything so red? It smells like… rusty nails or something." Lola turned around and glimpsed through the windows of the barn a gruesome sight. Several puercos hung upside down dripping blood.

"Oh Lola. Pay never mind. It's what they do here. They eat us, milk us, poke us. With no reverence at all." Lecche turned away with her tail to the barn. Even she could not bare to see the tragedy.

"Holy cow! I mean holy wow. I've never see this! How does this affect the humanos? They eat the puercos? Without even a prayer? I mean energy exchanges for energy, I get that, I also saw the processed SeeeReal fabrica, however, it seems part of the problem here on the planeta is how they nourish their bodies? Am I right?"

"Yes, I am afraid you are. It's not that easy though, Lola. There are so, so, so many humanos on the planet right now, many of them are starving to death. They need to eat, yet it's the way they cultivate us, process it. No empathy, no remorse, no union of spirit. That negative energy goes into their bodies and desensitizes it. But don't get too forlorn, there are many humanos waking up and eating beneficial foods   if they can just stop all that packaging nonsense!"

"Oh Lecche, I am so sorry for this," sighed Lola.

"And who's gonna be sorry for me? Eh?" A round faced man stuck his head out from the 2nd story of the barn. "Ya'll think it's easy to feed all the humanos. Somebody's gotta do it. I'm the Slotter-or. I don't like working for them corporAshuns, the bosses don't care, they just want more, more, more!!"

"Well, perhaps for now we could compromise? Just like Lecche offered, perhaps you could build an altar to the puercos, ask permission from the ancestors and engage some sort of ritual for the death of the beast?" Lola's heart was pounding. This all seem so upside down.

Slotter-Or heard the puercos rustling. "Ah gee. I like these critters. I do. More than humanos. Well,

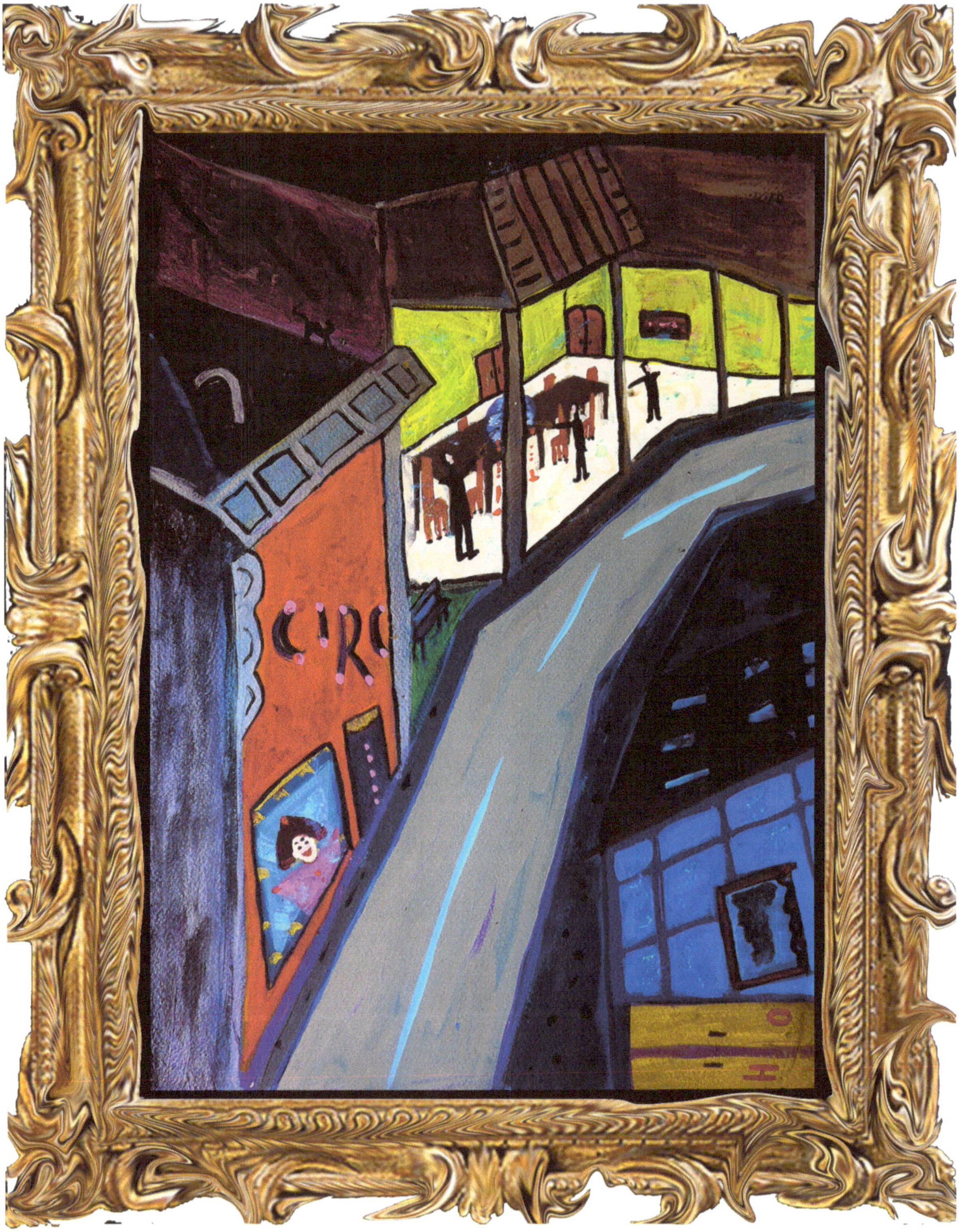

maybe I can do something different. Like you say. Tend to the spirit of 'em or something. Be more gentle."

"That's a good start. You don't want humanos eating the story of fear that the puercos had before death. If the being is at rest, it leaves with that in its blood and a better story and nourishment. Who are these bosses at the corporAshuns you speak of," asked Lola?

"They're in the citay. Why don't you go talk to them? Well anyway, nice to meet you, but I gotta get back to work." Slotter-Or disappeared into the darkness of the barn.

"They work so hard for so little, would you like some of my cheezy treats, Lola," asked Lecche?

After a small meal, Lola walked towards the citay. Heshe wanted to meet some of these bosses at the corporAshuns. Why would they want to destroy humanos and an entire planeta?

The steel glimmered and lights shimmered along the concrete boulevard. Lola peeked into the windows as heshe passed store after store after store of things and more things after those things. Along the wide avenue, Lola came upon a location with long, rectangular glass windows, it looked like a giant aquarium. Heshe stopped to observe what was happening inside. Lola heard voices through the gaps of the doors.

"We need more materials to build another skySkraper. We are the PatriaArcals and need to stay in control of the world's markets," said a man in a black suit.

"But the humanos are worried about the rivers and the oceans. Will it hurt the fish or the ballenas," asked another shorter man in a blue suit?

"Who cares? Build them another ocean? Extinction has always been a part of this planeta. What can we do? They need jobs. They want food. They want to move around the world for cheap. We give them what they want! Honestly, Gorgi, pick up one of those black shooting sticks and help us mark our next location," demanded the tall man in the black suit.

Then, to Lola's horror, heshe watched as the men aimed their black shooting sticks at a replica of Gaia on a long table. BOOM! BOOM! Pellets hit the round blue globe, while red streaks fell from the sides, like blood. It was blood! Life blood of the planeta dripping onto the ground. Lola's heart was beating so fast, they didn't know what to do. Appaulled, heshe stumbled down the street gasping. Lola burst into tears.

How could humanos be so contrary? Those at the sanctuario seemed kind, yet, this was a whole different breed. The patriArcals they had called themselves. Lola gazed hopelessly into a window at a nearby store. A manikin waved to Lola. Heshe recalled a distant memory and the lessons from the Urn of Desires, how those spirits had abandoned heshe in the citay. Lola shuddered to think that so many humans had succumbed, been hypnotized by the false prophets of desire and material wealth. Once again, the manikin waved at Lola, but this time more ardently, motioning heshe to join them.

Lola tapped on the window. There was a odd looking clownish girl with purple hair and a pink suit. "Hello? Hello? Can you hear me," inquired Lola?

"Yes! Of course! Pay them never mind. Their ship is sinking. They are on their way out, their idea of profits-at-all-costs! It's an old school. Hey, you look like you need to shake, shake it all off a bit. Am I right," asked the manikin?

Lola took a deep breath. "Yeah. I sure do. Got any ideas?"

"Well there's a dance hall down the street. It's a good place to unwind and maybe meet some new friends? It's a happy place for gae, qweers n transvesties and such…"

A memory flashed in Lola's mind of flashing coconuts and hundreds of humanos dancing during heshe's frightful night in the citay after the spirits from the Urn of Desire deserted Lola. "Um, are you sure? I went to a place in the citay a long time ago, humanos were dancing but it wasn't very friendly."

"Well, go then and just dance. Shake it up. Jiggle it off. Move it all out of your body. Give it a whirl.

Twirl. It can't hurt. Why not," coaxed the clown?

"Yeah, I guess, why not!" Lola lifted their head and winked at the clown and skipped off to find the dancehall.

---

*T*he sidewalk rumbled as Lola approached the dance club. A large neon and gold sign read 'Club Eksta SEE'. At the door, Lola was greeted by welcoming smiles. The place was gorgeous to behold, flashing lights of all kinds, mirrors playing tricks on the eyes, and a glowing dance floor. Lola couldn't resist. The clown was right, go out there and just dance. Lola shimmied and wiggled their thin body along with the others. A group of four beings came and surrounded Lola in their dance.

"Hi there! I'm Jump, and these are my friends, Twist, Swirl and Groove. Isn't this place a blast," shouted Jump?

"Yes! It is! Do you come here often," asked Lola?

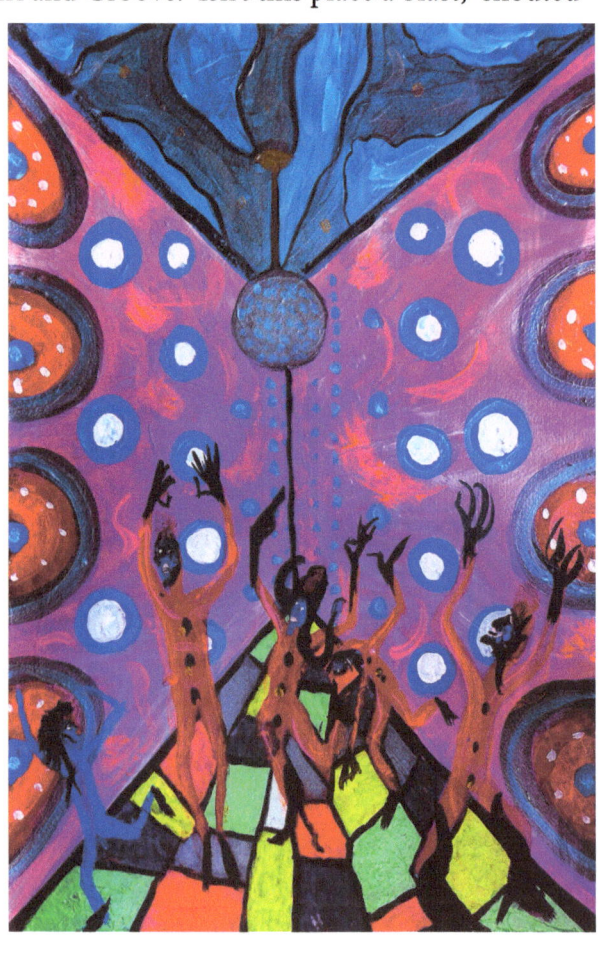

Jump motioned Lola and the others to the lounge area to take a break. "This is like our church. We come here to celebrate life and dance joy onto the planeta. It invokes the spirit of Sarah Tonen."

"I've never heard of a church, nor your spirit friend, Sarah Tonen. Tell me more, if you will," asked Lola? Heshe sat at a large round booth with the others and enjoyed the sights inside the extravagant nightclub.

"Wow, OK. A church is a place where those who are called can focus their thoughts and will towards a collective idea. It's been misused or perverted by groups who desire to control the path to the divine, but never mind that here. Sarah Tonen is a cousin to Sara Pheame. They both help your moods." Jump winked at Lola.

"I know Sara Pheame. I met the plant deva with the dragoneflies. I learned a lot about ah Day eN A. That's so cool we know some of the same friends." Lola smiled brightly at the others.

"We come here to connect to the ecstatica energy of being a humano and transcend all the depression of the outside world. So, you've never been to an actual religioso church? Tomorrow we can show you one. But for now, let's go dance!"

Lola remembered an old dream within a dream of dancing around the fires with other double-spirits…

---

*T*he church was ominous, yet stunning. It had sharp jagged points that pierced the sky. The windows were like none Lola had seen before on heshe's journeys. They were remarkably colorful with intricate designs. Lola approached the building somewhat apprehensively; heshe could feel unstable energies lurking.

"Psssst. Pssst. Well I'll be! Lolaboy! It's me, your old friend! Over here! Calusaris Layton Latento at

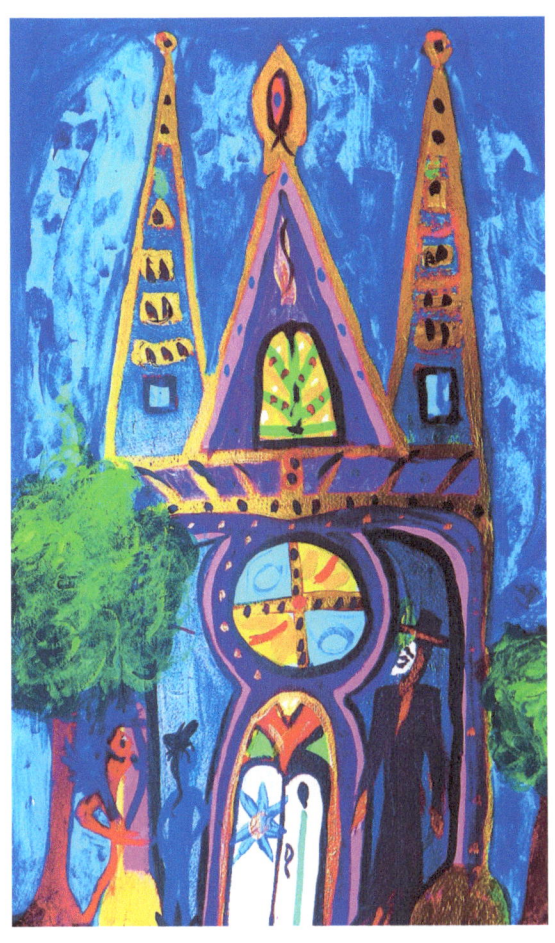

your service. I see you found one of the 'other' types of circuses for humanos. Hahaha," laughed Calusaris. His crimson body startled Lola as it sprang from the bushes.

"Oh yeah! Hello there. How's Loquatia and everyone at the Circo de Duendes," asked Lola?

"Ah you know, crey crey as ever. What brings you to this center of false profitsphets and their messy-onics influence. Looking for a new path to the divine? There's lots of these places on the planeta. Folks are obsessed with someone to lead 'em out onto the glory way to dios! Lawdy have mercy. Wars, Blood. Control. Worship me. But the buildings are something to look at, aren't they?" Calusaris pointed at the church.

"So, what do these places have that link humanos to a more balanced way of mind and heart? I don't get it." Lola gazed inquisitively at the patterned windows with images of humanos and animals and lightening— all sorts of things, but one was quite bewildering. It was a picture of a humano bleeding while hanging from a piece of wood.

"Ah well. At the core of that spectacular story, it was somewhat good natured. It was intended to show humanos that the divine benevolent source lived within them and inside every other living being on the planeta. It was an effort to get humanos to live with kindness and love. Then folks got nervous and jealous and created stories about the divine being… and it got very controlling, mean and well, actually pretty scary. If you didn't do what they said you ended up burning in flames or something like that…" Calusaris shuddered.

Lola couldn't believe their ears. The creators were mean? Violent? Controlling? Lola sighed. "Well, how do I get inside and see, so I can translate the energy and speak more wisely to my humano friends and the jaguar magicians. It feels like they are under a hexia spell."

"Sure, I can help with that. Lucius! Lucius! You around," yelled Calusaris?

A tall, lean man in a black robe with a chimney style black hat snaked towards them. He seemed wearisome and forlorn. "Calusaris, you've brought a friend. Hello, I'm ReverRabeye Lucius, Keeper of the Towers of Babble. Would you like to see inside? Glorious structures to build, yet it's infected with pretentiousness spirituality to a degree. Ah well, step inside," groaned Lucius.

The doors squeaked. Dust flew in the air. The nave was gigantic. Silent. Empty. Lola felt a hollowness. Something once, perhaps magnificent, had long left this place. Heshe touched the marble pillars. There was a waft moldy incense and death.

"Lucius, I come from another dimension, and I am here to learn of humanos day-to-day passages, so that I may mirror the vibrations of moving to another dimension of love and oneness. What happened to this place of spiritual viability," asked Lola?

"Hmm… doesn't surprise me you arrived here. The stories we tried to convey were of folks like you, we referred to them as saviors or in a reality they were more like avatars. Then? I'm not sure what happened.

Why did it got so controlling or vindictive? An obsession grew to control masses of humanos. Through stern dictates and an image of a brutal divinity, it became a source, a center to enable one gender to dominate another. Just look at the spires… large membranos of the masculino." Lucius pointed up at the golden pinnacles of sainthood. He shook his head and sat down in a slumber.

"OK, so the stories got juxtaposed. I was dancing with others that seemed OK with their creation story of the divino creators. And I was also at a sanctuario with others… but why is there so much fear about qweer, gender variants? I've come, in a way to liberate the jaguar magicians who are most certainly of the multi-sexed."

"Oh, my friend, these stories have been sliced, diced, contorted in such ways as to omit anything magical that prevented the leaderz their control… these places held the only truths. Complete malarkey! Everyone was taught to look outside themselves for reverence. And sadly those you speak of have been targeted for centuries. They represent the ultimate threat… to end or challenge the polarity of dual I tea. For their cerebros, and it is said and their corazons as well, are in fact more balanced and less harmful to Gaia." Lucius put his hand on Lola's shoulder and sat down next to him.

"How can I learn more about these books of thought. Do you know of any I can peruse," asked Lola?

"Well, yes, I do. Downstairs in a secret room. Come with me. It's time." Lucius guided Lola to the back of the church.

*T*housands upon thousands of books lined the walls of the musty chamber several levels beneath the main floor of the church. Lucius had taken Lola to the central library. He offered original texts were available for Lola to explore. All types of artifacts, bones, amulets, crystals, powders lined the shelves. It looked as though nothing had been touched for a very long time. Lucius left Lola alone to study.

Lola grabbed a tall book that was titled, Hermetics, Wizards, Alchemists & Time Travelers. When heshe opened the binding, a whoosh of spirits filled the air.

"We are the spiritus of long agoeth. What do you seek master Lola?" A screechy voice echoed and filled the room.

"Why has so much been blocked from humanos? I don't get why there is such abusive control that they would destroy the life force of the place upon which they need to survive? Even their leaders need a place, do they not," asked Lola?

"Ah. These are stories within stories. Not just of the realm of Gaia and her humanos. These are complexities that involve stories of many tribes within the stars. Whilst all are of the magnificent off spring of creativity from the ALL, there are energies that spiral with distinct karmic imprints. Gaiaic realms such as this Planet of Great Consciousness congeal into many forms of gathered polarizations of atoms. These all seek harmony as all energy desires. Yet, humanos have struggled with beings who have sought to control and abuse them for their sinister karmic release and other profiteering schemes."

"Have species such as theirs ever overcome such

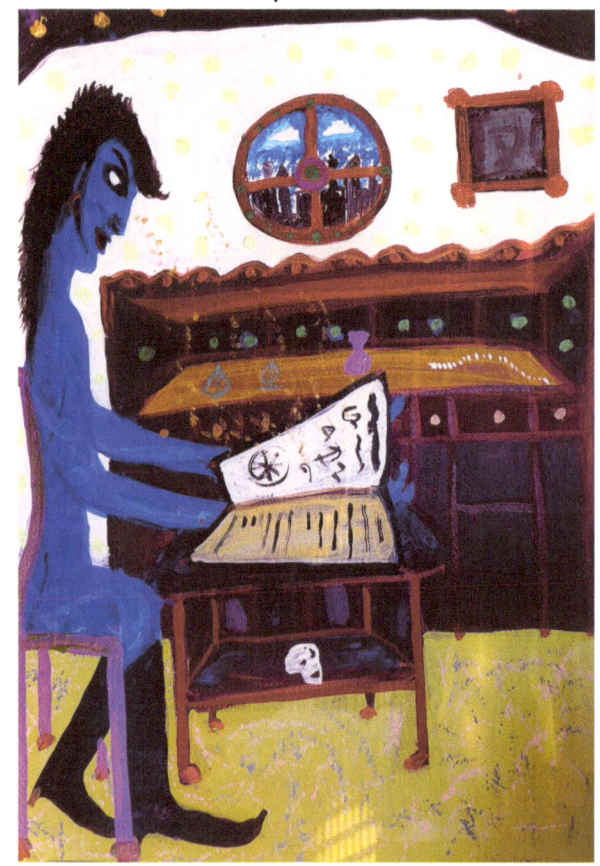

power? I mean, it feels like there is a vibrational quality to this planeta, it's readiness for ascensia, yet density holds it in a sort of mechanized pattern. How did others before them break free," asked Lola?

A skull on the shelf began to speak. "One cannot say that it is any one thing that liberates a place during its conscious evolution. However, it seems that when enough of a collaboration or focused will of any energy source leans towards a certain pattern it will unify for a time. Perhaps humanos will reach this tipping point."

"Thank you, I need to ponder this all." Lola stood up and tucked a few books under their arm. Heshe asked permission to borrow the books and left the church. Lola needed to escape for a moment. "Ok spirit, where to next?"

The streets of the citay were mostly empty. Lola longed for something to help heshe understand this aggressiveness in humanos. Back at the sanctuario, the RadFae had spoken about a cinemama where one could watch visual projections on a wall. That afternoon, as perchance Lola had come upon such theatrical display. Heshe entered the movie kingdom and found a seat towards the back. The screen came on and sad music filled the room. Within seconds startling blasts shook the floors. While it was from the cinemama's presentation, it seem ever so real to Lola. Heshe watched with a bulge in their throat as the story of warz engulfed the theatre. It was dreadful. Blood. Fighting. Screaming. Tears. It seemed endless terror. Never had heshe played witness to such destruction. How was this satisfying to humanos to watch such monstrosity as a form of entertainment? Just as Lola had that very thought, the film changed and an animated spirit arrived. Out of the screen came a demonia. Lola could see it, but it semed no one else noticed.

"Who…whooo are you?" Lola whispered to the giant beast who had now filled the entire theatre.

"I am Terroristam, the Perpetrator of Fear. They LOVE me. They pay millions of their silly dollars

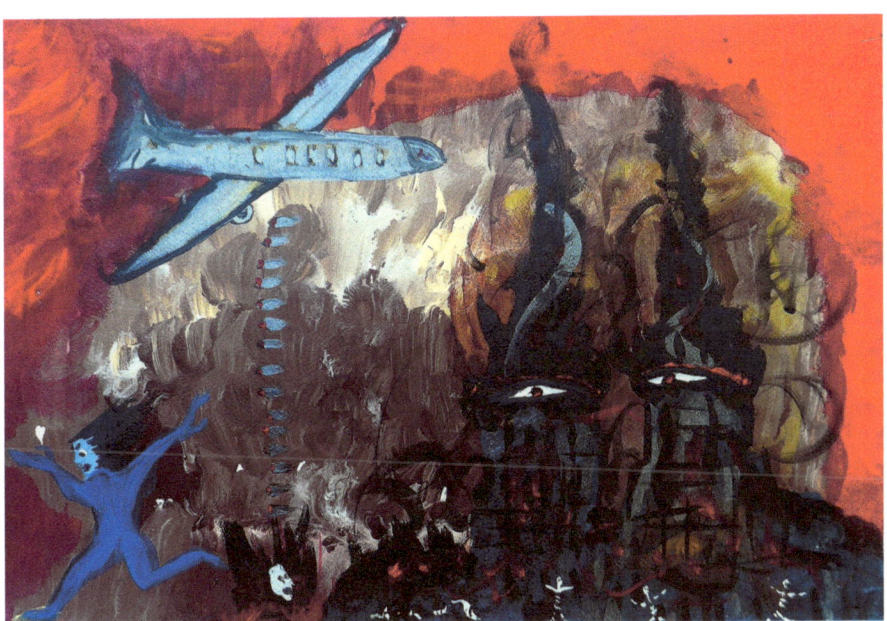

to reproduce images of pain and suffering. They worship my bombs. They would rather pay for this than to educate or to learn. Their governments are full of my energylings."

"But what a waste of energy, materials, lives?" Lola shook in disbelief.

"Ah, but my story proceeds humanos. We have thrived on many planetas, even destroyed their existence. We feed on the flesh of consciousness. It's important for us to control populations! Capow!" Terroristam returned to the screen, while other sinistros and gouleys fluttered in the rafters of the theatre.

Lola could see how these films were portals for demonias to pass onto humanos. It was a way to emphasize a certain dense vibration…keep humanos vulnerable… their cerebros numb and normalize such violence. The sounds continued to get more and more fierce from the film, until Lola could take no more. Heshe raced out of the cinemama.

Lola had not been this shaken in a long time. Their mind was spinning with horrible things. What had these energies done? Why had Gaia attracted such beastly figures? Why were humanos mesmerized by fear, reproducing it for entertainment?

Lola wandered into a small wooded area just outside the citay. Heshe laid down next to a tree to rest and to hopefully transmute what had just happened. Lola waited for something that generated joy.

The tree above Lola rattled its leaves. "Phoenix. Ocelotl. I think Lola needs a moment with you. Heshe's been exposed to the warz entities."

In seconds, they appeared. The All-Seeing-All-Knowing-Eye joined them.

"Ah dear. Yes. The interplanetary disruptions. The fierceness. The legacy of their aftermath and karmic debris is tumultuous to say the least. There is the state of compensation, a way to reach into a state of neutrality from the larger rhythms of the universe."

"Why don't we summon Guerrero Antiguo. Perhaps his energy can rid heshe of some of these frustratingly inherent karmic fragments from the cinemama.

Lola opened their eyes. Startled, yet relieved, heshe saw that they were joined by old friends. "Oh dear, did I do something to bring you all here? It's just holy wow, that film? Do they know what they are doing?"

"Some do. Lola. There exist on the planeta what are referred to as 'walkins' from other worlds that bring chaos and deliberately confuse humanos. Alas, we couldn't hide you from this, nor would it serve you to be hidden any longer from the delima of the universe. There are many worlds within worlds, possibilities within possibilities, yet the ALL knows the ALL and that ALL is perfect and imperfectly perfect. We have a friend we'd like you to meet, Guerrero, do you have anything to add to this story," asked Ocelotl?

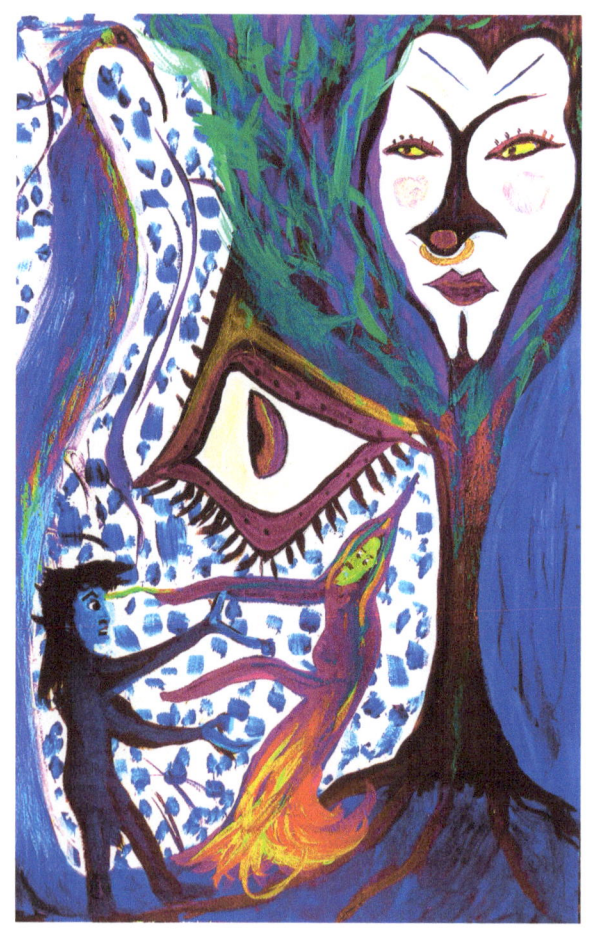

The ancient spirit warrior rose up and floated towards Lola. "It is troublesome, Lola, I wholeheartedly agree. Yet, sad to say, some of those wars, needed to happen. Not everything is easy to balance, and when something gets so agitated and advanced in a world that bring pain and strife, then yes, there is a like-for-like, and maybe the energy is matched to dispel it. Thus, the pendulum swings.

But I think Ocelotl and the others would like me to introduce to you the concept of the sacred warrior. The place of compensation. You can teach yourself to watch with neutrality knowing that the pendulum swings back and forth and that those degrees of swinging are sometimes large and significant and sometimes very small and seemingly insignificant.   It's not about becoming ambivalent, yet it runs alongside, there becomes a necessary feeling of non-attachment.   The ALL, as represented by this All-Seeing-All-Knowing Eye, knows what it does and does not know. It has purpose and it learns from its evolving. Yet, it does not need to evolve. This isn't about right or wrong, it is about energy trying to harmonize. And… when it sets into balance for a time, it is lovely. A volcano erupts and tosses boulders of rocks and flames kill vast swaths of terrain only to regenerate into lushness. This is not to say those wars, in 3-D are as grande as a volcano, especially when there is so much seduction of possibility." Guerrero sighed. "Oh dear, have I helped you in any way Lola?"

Lola took a deep breath, "Yes. You have. I have seen so many wonderful developments, although, it's as you offer, there is a grand motion in process to rebalance Gaia's realm."

Ocelotl spoke. "Lola, we shielded you from many things, but it is important for the growth of your empathy to mature into compassion for all things. You now see what it really takes for a jaguar magician to 'wake-up. Now get some rest, we are at your side, there's still some challenging things for you to experience."

The next morning, Lola was a bit more relaxed, yet wary. Heshe decided to stroll deeper into the woods and reflect on Guerrero's words. Neutrality. Compensation. Non-attachment. Wow this fixed state of 3-D was so genuine in its tangibility that heshe understood how difficult it was for many of the humanos to recover from the nature of its realness. As Lola walked, they noticed fewer and fewer trees and more and more remnants of stumps. They covered the landscape for as far as once could see like tombstones in a graveyard. Lola gasped. The landscape changed dramatically. Suddenly there were no more trees at all just a barren field of tree corpses. Heshe heard loud blasting noises coming from the distance. Some sort of machine was crushing and moving the fallen trees.

Lola hopped up onto a stump and took it in. Ok. Neutral. Non-attachment. They need wood for their buildings, right? But my goodness, to just denude an entire region? Lola felt tears come to their eyes.

Wisps of spirits began to fill the air. One by one they rose from the remains of the trees. They sang a chorus to Lola.

Bones of trees.
We are the bones of trees
And we have a plea
Once upon a time
We covered the land from sea to sea
And they us blind
Brothers and sister take heed
Without us there will be a fuss
For no oxygen will come from us!

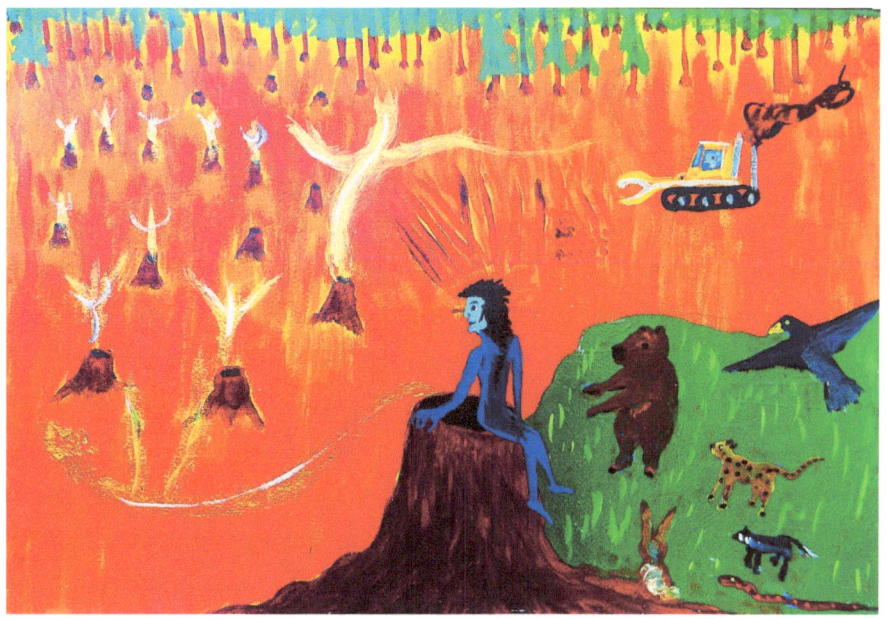

While the tree spirits shared their lament, several tranimals gathered around Lola.

A large bear approached Lola. "My friend, fret not. Look behind us? There is green, renewal, regeneration coming with each breath. It is true many of the humanos have lost connection to the forest folk as kin. But so too, many are restoring their relationship as well. That is the faith we spread now. Turn around, and come with us to another part of the forest and meet some of our friends."

*S*oon they reached a lovely clearing in the woods. Flowers and bushes were blooming and birds tweeted in the branches above. Lola laid down on the grass with HareHare and the Bear and others. A lovely song could be heard from behind a large tree.

Just then, a wild looking being jumped out into the clearing and danced a jig.

"Hello Lola and my dear friends! I'm PinPan, an elfin being from the 'Once Woods'. Oh, sweet Lola, so distraught you've become with the images on Gaia. My tribe comes from a 4-D realm which we call, Lyrica. Let me show you how to blend or synchronize energy through song. The music of the spheres. You may remember this from the blueberry faeire Auntie Oshedante?"

PinPan offered Lola the lute. "Go a head try it. Make a wish and blow into the pipes," giggled the elf.

Lola blew into flute. An amazing foray of notes fluttered into the air. Lola was playing music. Immediately, heshe could feel its warmth encircle the forest.

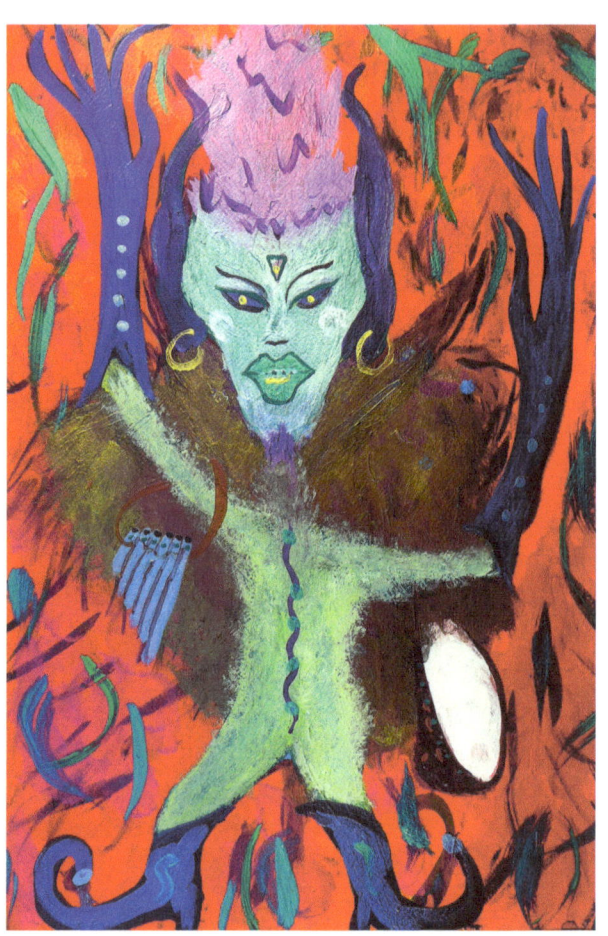

"Everything around you has a song. A note. A vibration. Together they emit harmony. Indeed, that deforestation has a low vibration like a deep growl. But I encourage that when you walk upon the Gaia transformational plane, that you take into consideration methods to remove the cords of the doubt matrix. You've done that before in the Pyramid of Remembrance. Now use that same skill here and mirror this out to the humanos to dispel and transmute apathy."

*T*hen someone or something laughing hysterically and jumped into the clearing.

"Is this a party? OMG, PinPan! You didn't invite me?" A sprite blue elf tackled and tickled PinPan to the ground.

"Ac Pa Da…ssss ss sss stop it… I'm going to pee myself," laughed PinPan.

The two stood up and shook the leaves from their clothes. "Everyone this is my friend Ac Pa Da &*% (a weird sound came from PinPan's mouth). And yes, the *&^% sound is part of his name. This one is the queen of games!"

PinPan motioned for everyone to sit down. "So, Ac, whatcha got up your sleeve? Could it be… could it be a game?"

"Hm. Maybe. Maybe not." Ac Pa Da *&% threw several small black and white blocks into the air. "It's all about the throw of the dice and how they land!"

The blocks fell to the ground. Each had a series of arranged dots on them.

"These are dice. Lola, they toss em around to sharks in Lost VEghast, a huge citay in the humanos playbox. Of course, I don't mean literal tiburones. I mean those that have a knack, an eye for numbers,

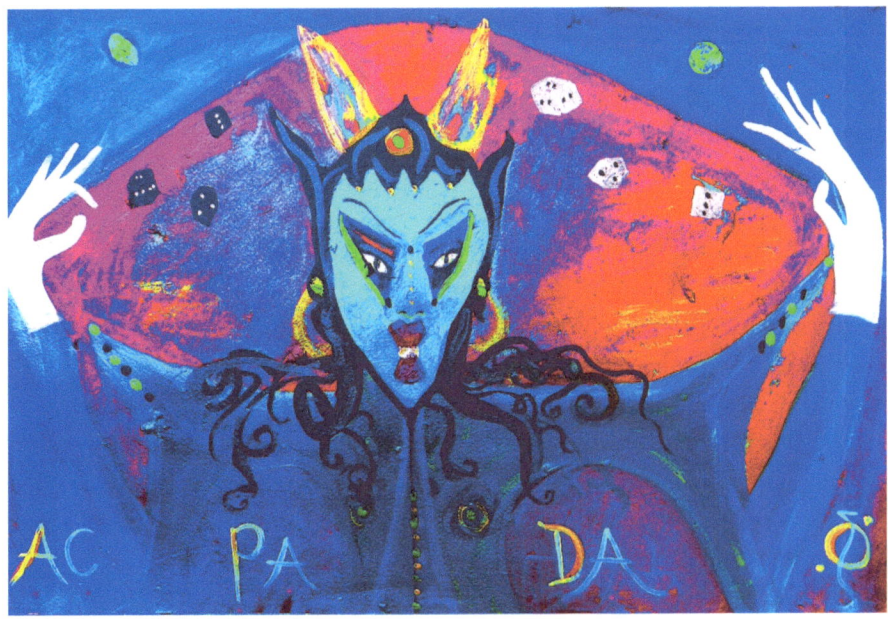

chance, luck, possibility… some would say odds. Go ahead Lola, roll the dice see what you get!"

Lola tossed the di into the air and they fell to the ground. Plop. Plop. Small puffs of dust rose when they landed. "It looks like I got seven dots."

"Ahah! A Mystic portal. Just like PinPan's lyrical tunes have a vibration, so do numbers. So, Lola take some advice. Life is like a game of sorts. No winners or losers. But there is a game. You have a set of skills and talents. Bedazzle em. Bewild them. When the going gets rough, sing a song, hum it back into equilibrium. When you see something that don't feel right see it as a game. Numbers are easy cuz they're everywhere. If you know the story, or energy or magnificence of a certain number you can play the game of numbers wherever you are. Think about that for a moment."

The group sat around and played games into the night until Lola curled up and fell into a deep sleep.

In the morning, the sun splashed through the trees causing Lola's eyelids to flutter. A new day. Lola looked around. The others had scuttled off to their holes, caves or wherever they slept, he supposed. Ah well. It was a fun night of games and songs. Lola was feeling lighter of heart. OK. Well then, so much of this realm would require a lot of transmutation and transcendence.

Lola hummed and strolled deeper into the forest. It became mountainous.

Kaboom! Kapow! Bam! Lightening lit up the sky.

A storm was coming, I better take cover, thought Lola. Heshe ran to find a cave or any kind of shelter. The sky turned a blazing orange-red.

"Yarrrrr. Take that, you silly machine! Bizzzowwww you crummy little destroying thing without a cause. No heart in ya!" Someone was shouting on the other side of the trees.

Time after time, Lola was rattled by the noise coming from a clearing in the trees. A giant wumun dressed in a lovely flowing pink gown was waved her sword in the air shouting curses.

"Lola. Don't worry I see you! Hang on a minute! There's one more of them buggars… I wanna get… weeeeee…" KaPOW! A bolt of lightning sent a bulldozer into the air.

"Holy wow. Are they gonna be hurt," shouted Lola?

"Nah, just bruised, mostly stunned. They'll wake tomorrow and wonder what happened. But their machine is destroyed. Good, you made it this far. I'm Hella, by the way. I have control over the fires of life. At least these ones. She took her sword and blew on it before sheathing it.

"What has happened here?" Lola gazed upon the landscape at charred trees and shattered rocks.

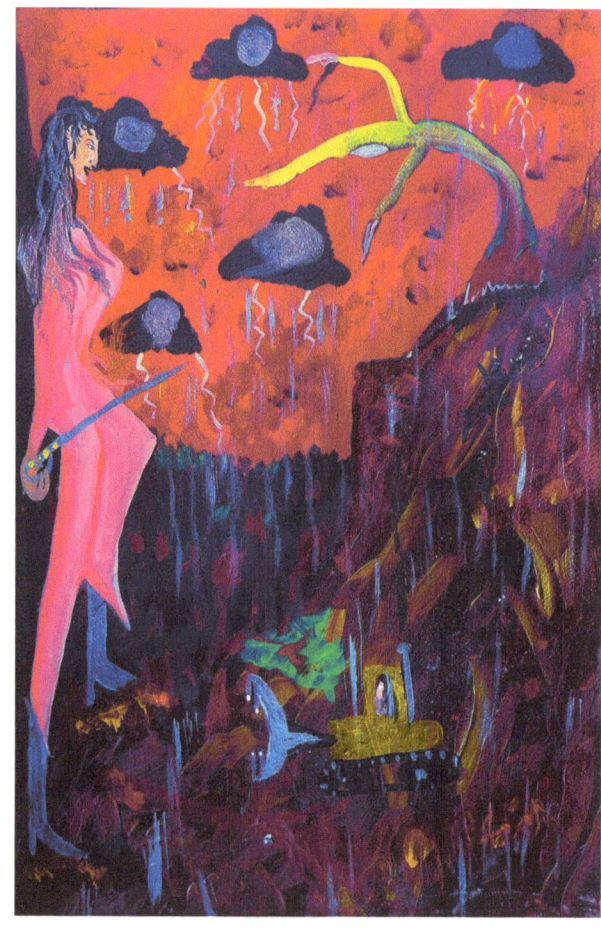

"Well, I guess your guides thought it might be good for you to see some of the other powers at work on Gaia. Of course, the humanos just think it's a cyclone or a fire or something natural, yet, likely it's me or one of my kind. See this sword? It's one of the swords of truth. Remember when you used the Blade of Acceptance? You saw its power over the Phantoms, Skeptica and other mayhem. Anyway, one swing of this blade and it cuts through the veil of deception really quick."

"Yeah, I remember those times. But how does this help? What you're doing," asked Lola?

"Ah, it's the power of regeneration. Like yer buddy, Phoenix. Rising up from the ashes, new worlds are formed."

"Why don't *you* lead the humanos then," inquired Lola?

"Nah, I can't cross over into their presence. Anyway, I think you should go meet one of their leeeederzz. Take that road there, and it leads to a place called Wash Da See and in there lives a Prez A Dent. Ask him what he thinks about control." Then a loud Pop! Hella had burst into flames and disappeared into smoke.

So much mayhem on this planeta. So many beings involved. Wowza. How am I ever gonna wake the jaguar magicians? Lola wandered down the path to which Hella had pointed. Suddenly, giggles came from everywhere. Above Lola was laughter. To the side. Behind heshe. Below. What was going on?

"Looooooooolaaaaaa! I know what you need! You need a good old-fashioned CirCuss. Laugh at all the crap. Did you know laughter brings enzyminios into your stomach and then up to your mind until you feel good? Now, do yo-self a favor, find a CirCuss as soon as you can and Laugh! Laugh! Laugh! Fear and dismay will have no power over you when you giggle!

Giggles, wiggles and squiggles.
Twirls, whirls and swirls.
Never stop the laughter.
Because you know what's after,
The fun, the surprise!
The feeling of being wise!

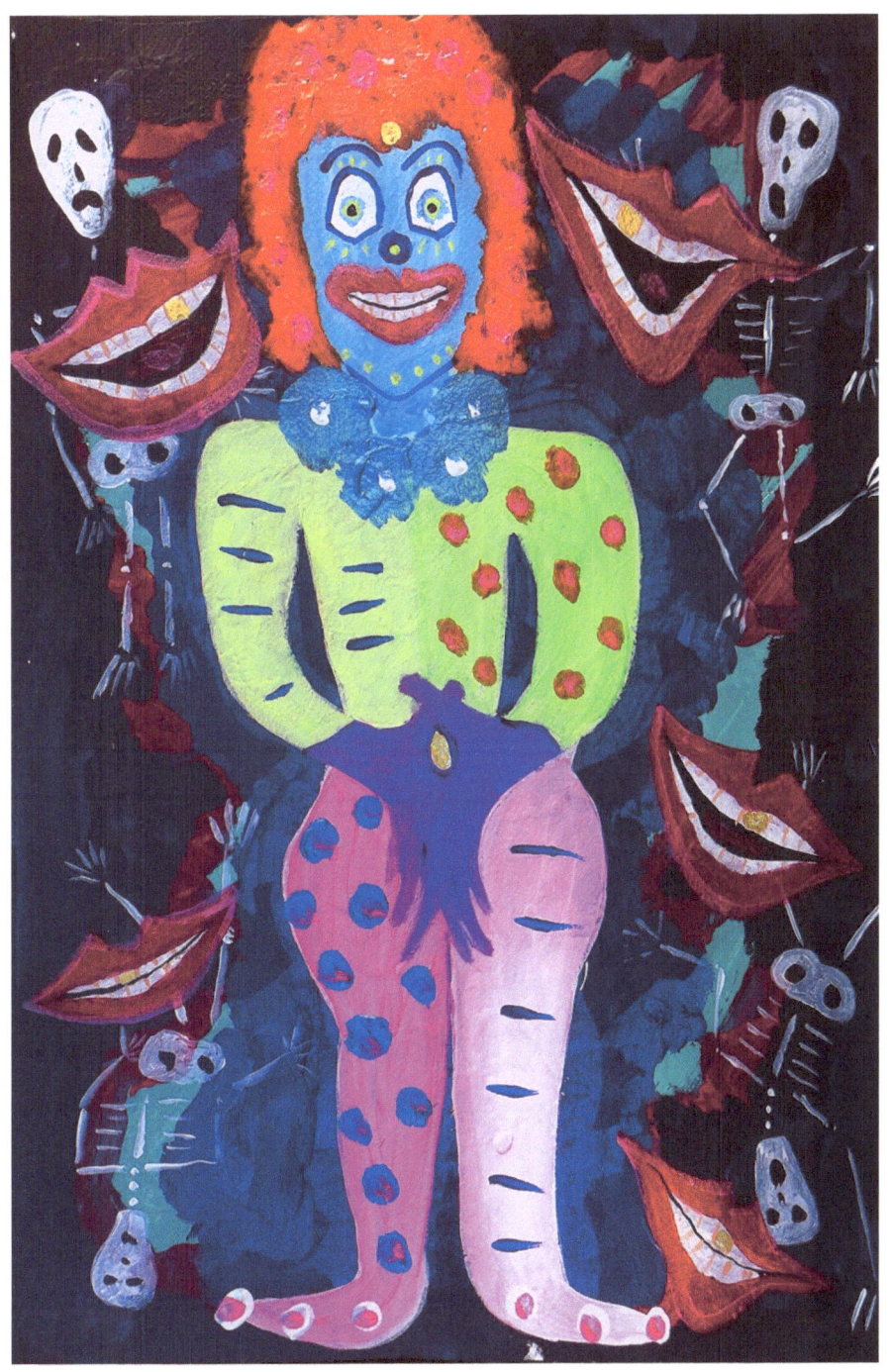

The elves had put Lola on a road that was actually a time portal. Therefore, heshe emerged from the laughter of the saKred Klown and arrived directly into WashDSee. At first, Lola observed the surroundings from behind a tree. There was an enormous white house with innumerable men in black suits roaming the grounds. Many of them carried pistolas. Lola heard the sound of crunching gravel beneath tires and watched as a limmonzene parked in front of the grounds. A man jumped out and pointed a long armament in every direction. Then, he escorted a tall, lean somber man from the car into the house.

After a few minutes, the armed men dispersed and the scene was quiet. Lola saw SunSol setting behind the huge, imperial building. "Hey there Sol. What do you think? Should I just go up and there and say hello? There were all those men with weapons."

"Dear heart. This is another world, you know that. There is a lot of paranoic energy on this plane, and especially here around their leeeeederzz. It's become quite a deception of whom they 'elect' as guardians. Rarely have they placed a humano who governs from the heart. But, back to your question, I will put a trance upon the land and you can pass unharmed. Go directly to the door. You deserve to have an audience with him. His name is Sir Romano Greco Egyptom. Good luck!" SunSol gazed vigilantly upon the horizon and radiated a calm energy across the land.

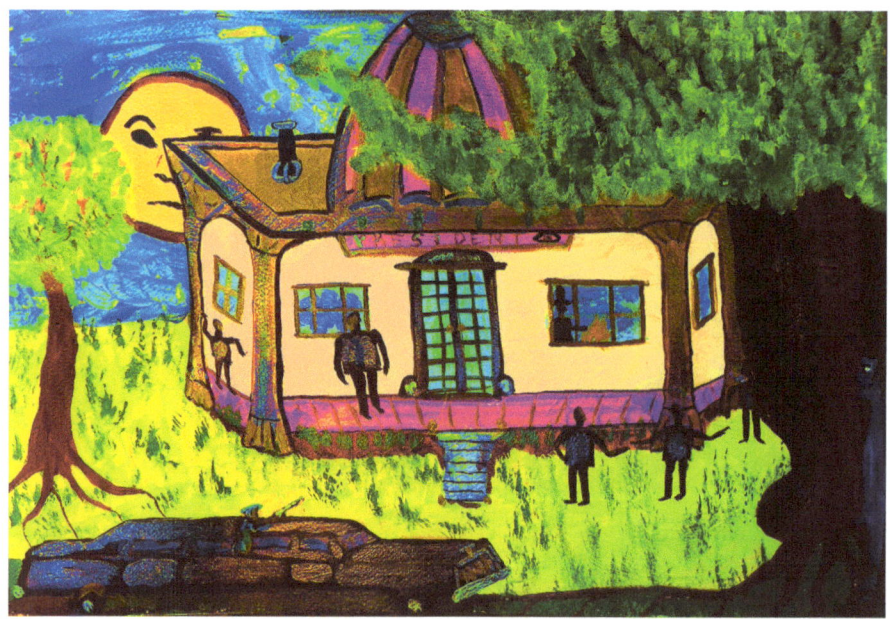

Lola bounded up the steps eager to meet the Prez. Heshe knocked on the door and heard floor boards squeak as someone came to the answer the call.

"Good Evening, young-un. How can I help you?" The Prez had been placed in a trance along with the others which enabled Lola to enter without the usual fear factors.

"Thank you, I'll just take a moment of your time, if you please. I'd like to discuss with you the plight of leeeederships on the planeta. I am Lola of the original Selva. What I have seen is so out of balance, that you must know the planeta cannot handle much more stress without collapse." Even though Lola's heart skipped rapidly, heshe felt a rush of boldness.

"Ah, sit down, then. I'll share some stories with you." The Prez sat on a pearl couch and poured a cup of tea for himself and Lola.

The room was filled with images of past leeederz. Lola felt them watching the meeting. Some looked dismayed, others shocked, while some seemed pleased. They were all acting as a witness counsel.

"Well first off, I wish I could say I earned this right, as some of my predecessors did, yet I feel compelled to tell you that my position was bought and paid for like a product in a store. I suppose they wanted someone who was intimidating…do I scare you?" Romano's brow furled as he looked at Lola for a response.

"No. You do not scare me. However, your governance confuses and dismays me. I have seen the forests cut. The piles of debris from the Toss-Aways, and the demonias released from the cinemamas. This is all discouraging fallout from your leeedership, sir." Lola stood tall, these guys needed to listen!

"Oh dear. Those are not accomplishments to be proud of, are they? Long ago, it was a Prez's duty to provide safety and, well, a fatherlier concept. A proud Dad. You see in this position, folks force their will—if that is even possible upon the mass humanos. Sadly, the wisdom has been cut off from this position. However, like the energy of the Ramgoaters, I understand more each day through experience that I must rule with more compassion. The corruptivos are massive with their influence. It is up to the humanos out there to call us out and hold us to better intentions and good will." Romano stood up.

"See these predecessors? It took endurance, determination, and mostly, courage to hold this position. Not everyone has or had it. Myself included." The prez shook his head.

"Sir, with respect, it feels that one may need to align themselves with the sacred universal laws. Not the religioso aspects, but more like the common initiatives. Those that recognize all life as equal and important, all love is love, and that with power comes great responsibility to maintain balance." Lola stood their ground. Heshe realized that the leeederz of the planeta would need to tend the equilibrium without sucumbing to the temptations of greed and unruly control. To speak with a leeeder may not happen again.

"My friend, you would do well as a Prez. Integrity of the leeederships are not the best. Yet. There is movement to restore honor to these positions. Mind and heart. Assertiveness and confidence with self-control… I get it. I've mastered a lot of obstacles to get here, I feel compelled, after your visit, to review the tactics of our governance. And, during the next time when there is a gathering of leeeeederzzz on the planetas, I will defy those that wish to purchase my truth. Instead, I'll drive forward a new direction for solutions that benefit all and radiate love." The Prez smiled shyly. "My word, did I say that?"

"You did, and I know in my heart you will do well. The trees are watching, the birds are listening, the dolphinas can feel you. They will also support you energetically. If I may add, spend more time alone in the forests or by the sea and breath deep. I must go now. I wish you well and thank you for your consideration to change." Lola stepped out into the evening.

Sunsol winked at heshe before setting into the night sky.

*L*ola decided to take saKred Klown's advice and find a Cirkus. Heshe wandered into a field outside of WashDSee. There it was! In the distance stood a glorious, sapphire, emerald and crimson tent that blossomed like a flower from the field. Lola raced toward the CirKuss.

SaKred Klown waved at Lola to join her beside the ticket booth. Then, to Lola's amazing surprise Magian Purpol had also arrived. If that wasn't enough, Lola looked up at the tent's pinnacle and saw Loquatia, Mistress of Misteries as she nodded her approval of the guests.

"Oh. This is wonderful! Good friends. And look, here comes SwanSong."

The elegant, white aviary waddled forward and stood in front of the tent honking its joy.

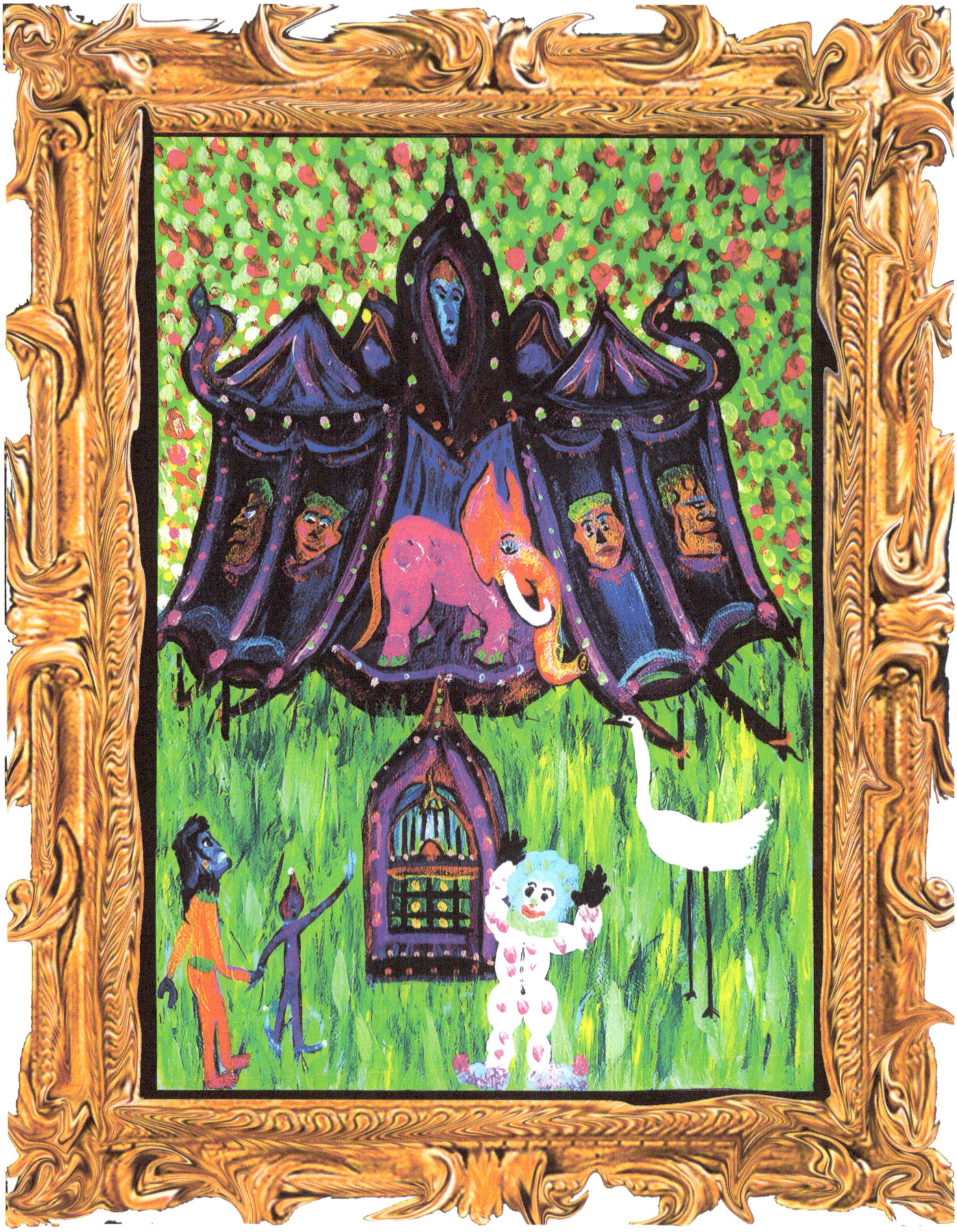

Cirkus Twirkus

Flip Flap!

Aroo Aroo!

Step beyond the line

And it feels so fine.

Make merry

With the Faeries

Swinging high

Don't ask why?

Swinging low

Welcome to our show!

As the flaps opened a giant pink elefant poked its head out. "I am Ganashea remover of all obstacles. Step inside! Come inside one and all. Illusions, but no delusions!" Bells rang and horns blew announcing the start of the show. Lola and the others rushed into the structure.

The CIRC theatre was much more than elegant to say the least, it was downright magical! Two large ruby and gold pillars framed the stage. Lola, Purpol, saKred Klown and SwanSong sat in the front row waiting anxiously for the show to begin.

Loquatia announced that the MC that night would be, Mago Marvavilla.

"Oh my! I know Marvavilla! How cool! A master mask-a-tier," exclaimed Lola!

Marvavilla was dressed in a luminescent blue suit with a tall pipe hat on their head.

"Greetings one and all, Elves, Wizards, Magicians, humanos and anyone who can hear me! Tonight, we bring you my friends Whimsy Flimsy, Spectaculata and more! Without further adieu…" Marvavilla clapped their hands and the curtains opened. There was a flash, smoke and Titire descended in a swinging silver chair.

"If you pull my string I'll do anything you want… I am a puppet you know. Watch this! I can dance on thin air." They flew back and forth on the swing.

Flimsy Whimsy came out holding a giant mask. "Seems like ya'll addicted to the masks. So I thought I'd bring the biggest one. I'll call it the 'mememe' mask. Who am I? Who do I want to be? Who do YOU want me to be? Tisk, task the masks we weave. I am a this! I am a that! And poof back to stardust we go!"

The theatrics continued and Lola laughed and giggled with the others throughout the entire show.

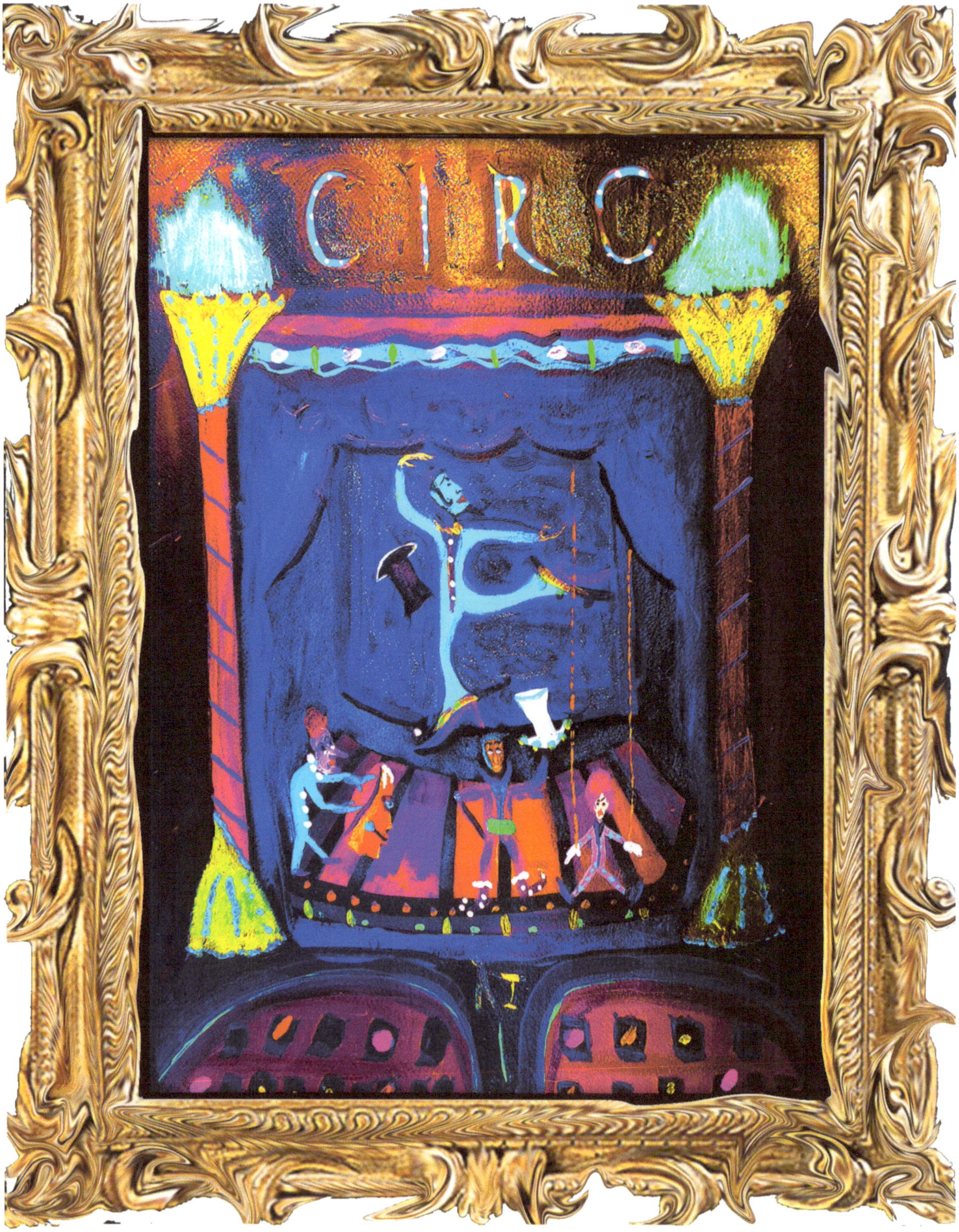

"*M*any times, the audience is a stationary arena we project onto. Yet I know better, you are the stage and we are the squirmy audience. Life is a stage is it not? Who do YOU cast in your show? And with that in mind, I'd like to bring out our final artist, Bluzona and her dancing, musical spiders!"

The image of Zuvuyana, Grandmother Aracnia flashed in Lola's memory. Weaver of time indeed, but now? Bluzona pounced onto the stage with several musical instruments.

"Well hello time travelers! I am humbly joined by our master weavers, Synth, DL, Dope and Trippy, the amazing, dancing, musical spiders! Quite the addition to the tribe of aracnia, I'd say." A blue spider joined them holding a golden harp. The other spiders each held a guitar, a flute and a fiddle.

Pitter patter patterna
Geomathico formulations
Of such sensations
Forming this-n-that
Could it be a bat?
Oh the shapes we create
In our mind's gates
Be careful of the though
The one you man naught ought!

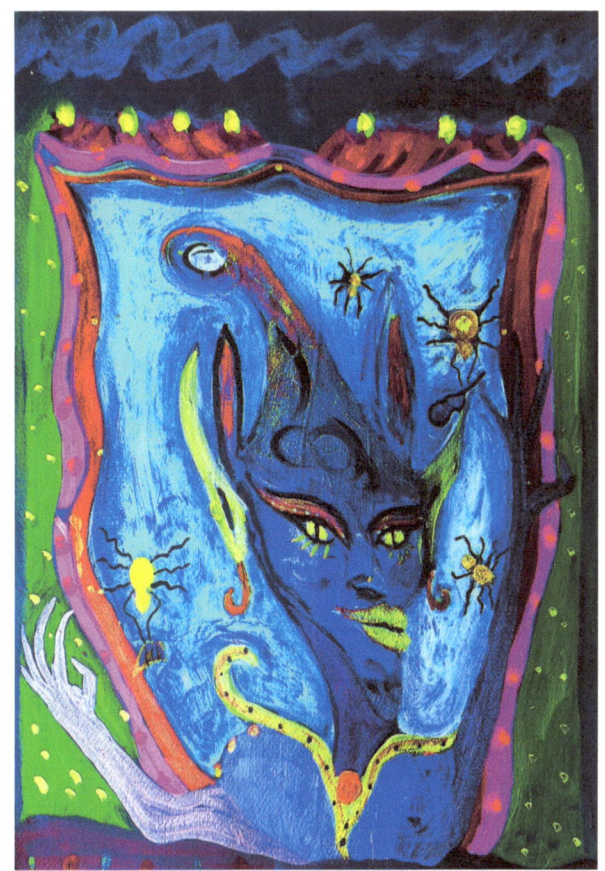

Lola was in bliss, taken back to the days of the Selva. Heshe looked to either side. Who were these amazing characters I cast in my dream walk on the planeta. Applause and gratitude filled the air as the final score brought the show to a close. The curtains were pulled shut with a woosh. Lola tiptoed backstage to say hello to Marvavilla and perhaps meet Bluzona.

"Hey Marvavilla! Wow, that was so cool," stated Lola.

"Oh hey! Come meet Bluzona!" Marvavilla grabbed Lola's hand.

"Well hello charmer! Thanks for witnessing the magic. Did you like our web we spun," asked Bluzona?

"I did, and would love to collaborate with your magic in weaving kindness and compassion on the planeta… with the jaguar magicians," offered Lola.

"Yes of course, we must! We shall!" Bluzona disappeared into the shadows of backstage.

*W*hile backstage, Lola noticed a gorgeous, laced canopy towards the back. It was occupied by three very exotic looking feminina humanos. One of them waved at Lola and motioned heshe to join them.

"Well hello there! We heard there was a jaguar wizard in the house. Purrrrfect. Never fear, I don't bite. I'm Opia, and these here are my sisterz, Frankensensia and Myhrrlotta."

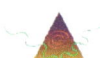

"Hello. I was quite enchanted by your flying dance tonight." Lola gushed.

"Why thank you! Yes, we learned that talent from our ancestor jipseaz. The wanderers. We come from the Kasbah. Our lineage would roam throughout the desert of the stars." Opia sighed. "Sadly, there are many of our tribe who are discarded as troublesome. There are those in the planetasphere whom live like us but don't want to…stashed in tents like piles of trash next to a rapid-roadway. Ah… well."

"Hey sis, lay off the smoke. You're depressing our guest. Shall we dose the magus with one of our scentaliscious experiences? Hm?" Myhrrlotta reached on to a shelf and pulled off a lovely bottle with a strange balloon-like thing on top.

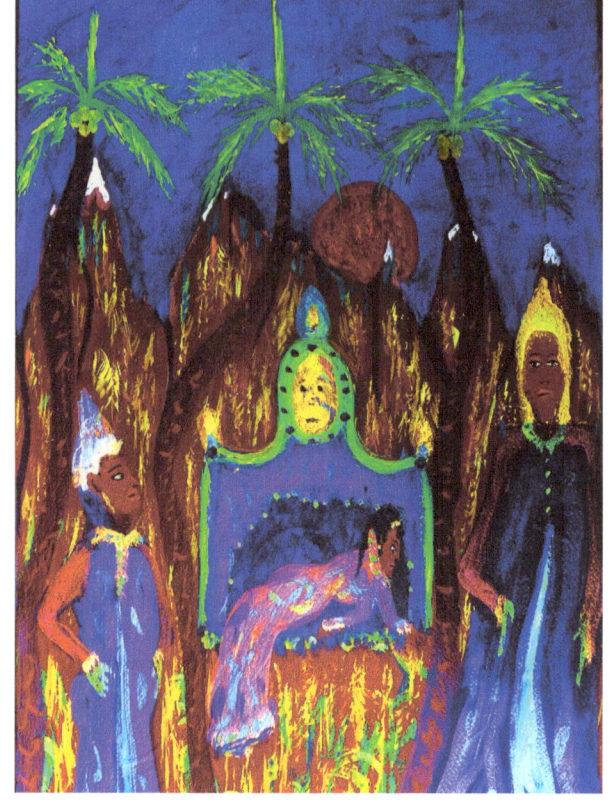

"Lola, your friend, Marvavilla shared that you haven't been in our realms for long. We call you a 'walk-in'… one of the good ones… hmph. We travel from show to show and in doing so we gather floras and herbas from all over the planeta. Then, we stir them into our golden cauldron with a bit of this and that and alkemia, then poof!" Myhrrlotta sprayed a violet liquid into the air within moments Lola relaxed and heshe's heart fluttered.

"Wow that smells incredible! What is that," asked Lola?

"It's one of our elixiras of the olfactoria. Did you know that these tiny molecules I just misted into the air travel directly into your brain? In seconds, they cause quite the party in your mind… changing the chemistry for beneficial results. Lavendula is a good one, isn't it? Wait till I offer you rosemaria." Myhrrlotta reached for another bottle.

"Slow down sis. However, she is right. We want to gift you with some of our essences to take with you, help you in a tight spot and change the illusion. They may help you awaken other jaguar's like yourself. Who knows?" Myhrrlotta plopped down into a pile of pink pillows. "Aw well, lovely Lola, we need to rest, why don't you curl up and rest as well, there's plenty of room."

Lola went to find Marvavilla and slept next to their friend.

The next day, Lola said goodbye to the cirKuss friends and again made way into the forest. Heshe found a handsome tree being and sat next to it and listened to its heart.

"So, master arbol, how are the trees doing? Honestly? Please, tell me what you can. I've seen the destruction and had several counsels with the tranimals and Hella."

Branches wiggled as the tree awakened from Lola's summons. "Hhhmmm. Truth to the maple trees! Like myself, they bring the magic of steadfastness and there are those that stay in one place for a long, long time. I've been in this forest for about 3000 years. We've been chopped for wood, paper and fuel. We give and give and they take and take. What can I say?" The maple tree tilted toward the west. "Hey out there! Forget-me-nots? You there? Come help me with this query."

Lola watched as several funny looking bluish-green beings popped out from behind tree after tree for as far as heshe could see.

Bring on the weather
Birds of a feather
Send in the rains
And end all the pains
Breathe deep
Awaken from your sleep
Call back the oxygen
Before this all ends!

"Thank you. I get it. I'll do everything I can to help humanos plant more siblings of your kind. Mmmmm oxygena." Lola heard a rustling nearby.

"Psst. Psst. It's me Ocelotl. I want to see how you're doing?" The magical felina jumped from behind a bush.

"Hey old friend, to be honest, it's a lot. All of it. Sometimes I just want to fly out of here. And some of it, is so amazing to behold, like the cirkuss, the RadFae…" Lola slumped over a bit in exhaustion as they shared concerns with the teacher.

"Well Lola, you hold quite a calling. Starseeder you are. With my voice, I remind you of the deep integrity you hold and mirror. You carry with every breath in and each exhalation out the depth of sovereignty for all beings. Carry these with you always, in all ways on your walkabout. Come with me, if you will. There's a place of replenishment that awaits you. There are some amazing secret places on the planeta…even in the realm of 3-D they still exist."

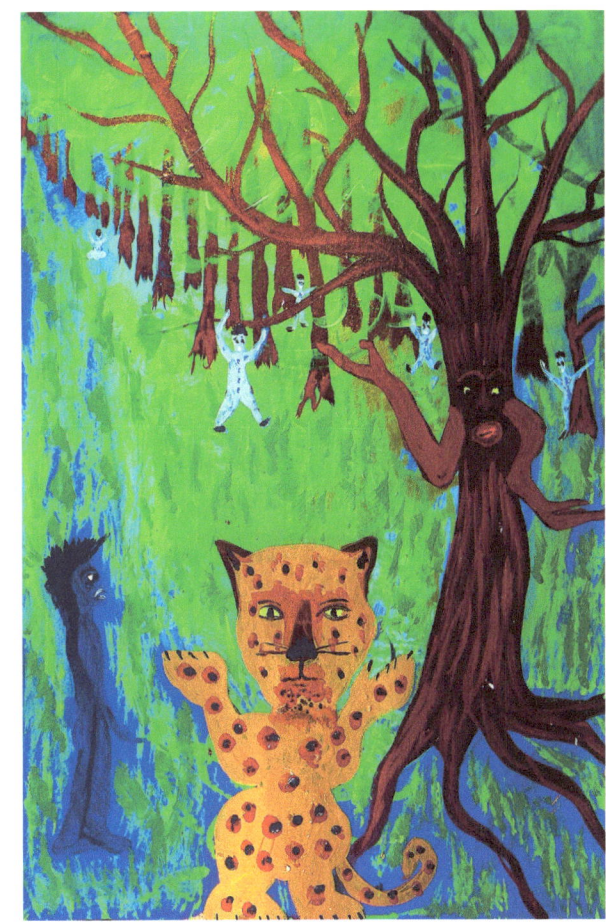

They walked for a long distance. Through steep ravines, rocky hills and along rushing rivers. Lola trusted Ocelotl to take heshe wherever was needed. It was true, while Lola was holding up endurance, there were times when heshe could practically bare no more of the wild chaos of humanos.

Around a bend, they swiftly revealed themselves. Lola's skin tingled. It was clear, wherever they were going was filled with spirits. Heshe could feel them already dancing around in the etherica.

They approached the top of a knoll and there it was…the most magnificent lake Lola had ever seen. Heshe gasped at its beauty. The view took Lola's breath away. The air was so sweet, clear, so pure that heshe could literally taste its vitality.

They descended in silence. Across from the lake was the largest mountain Lola had ever seen. Its height seemed to extend and touch the stars. Magenta, violet, rose, gold, green, it shimmered as much as the lake. Lola looked down at the waters and gasped.

"Oh my! Look at my reflection. The mountain. In the Lake. I've never seen such beauty," Lola whistled their joy.

"Shhh… Listen. She speaks. The Mountain too." Ocelotl put a finger to his mouth.

"Some come here to ask relevant questions. What is the World Mountain? It is a place where creators gather. In this lake, one replenishes their souls. Life is remembered here as immortal—even as it destroys itself. Some say the 'select one's' are the only one's who make it here, but everyone is a 'select one'. This is the place to communicate with all worlds. With the ALL. Every element and each of the parameters of the universal order are reflected from this holy mountain into the lake. In turn, she amplifies the energy one gives to it. Axis Mundi, this mountain is all mountains in all places and planes. Even the disjointed places join here. This is antiquity and future. All things are seen here. Nobody knows where this mountain is and yet everyone knows."

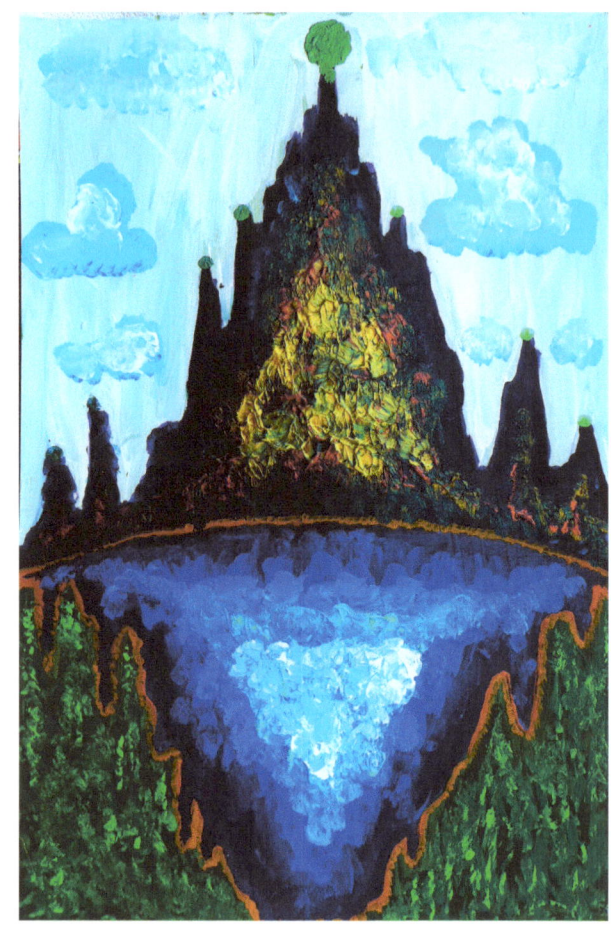

Ocelotl continued to channel the message. "There is nothing to climb here. Nowhere to descend. Now, drink from this ambrosia water and breath deep the fresh air and replenish yourself. Take no mind to the heathenism, barbarism, it is already history. Take this wonder back to the people. The humanos as you call them, fill them with this replenishing magic. For soon, they will be all be called to ascend. New levels of consciousness are ready. Help lift them up…. Even when they think they can no longer maintain."

Lola took a giant gulp of air and dove into the water. Then, like a flying dolphina, heshe flew to the top of the holy mountain.

"I am! That I am! That I AM," shouted Lola!

The walk down was not as easy, though Lola managed to do so without slipping. Meanwhile, Ocelotl had disappeared while heshe had jumped into the lake. Lola felt completely revitalized. As heshe continued on their path, Lola heard voices coming from inside a cave. Curious, Lola meandered into the large rocky crevice. There was a greenish glow. Five lanky magicians stood around the fire and debated. They wore opalescent robes of various shades. There arms shook in the air and dropped with disgust. What were they debating? Lola stepped closer to eavesdrop.

"Come on and join us! No need to hide! We could use all the help we can get to sort out our quandary! The confounded humanos! Evolution, revolution or de-evolution, what do you think, Helba?"

"For goodness sakes, er… excuse us. We are the hairOfants, keepers of the schools thought. Wisdom perhaps. You are the Lola we hear of?" Melbo extended a hand for Lola to join them next to the magical emerald flames.

"Yes, I've just come from Merutua, the Holy Mountain where I was with Ocelotl." Strangely, Lola felt no

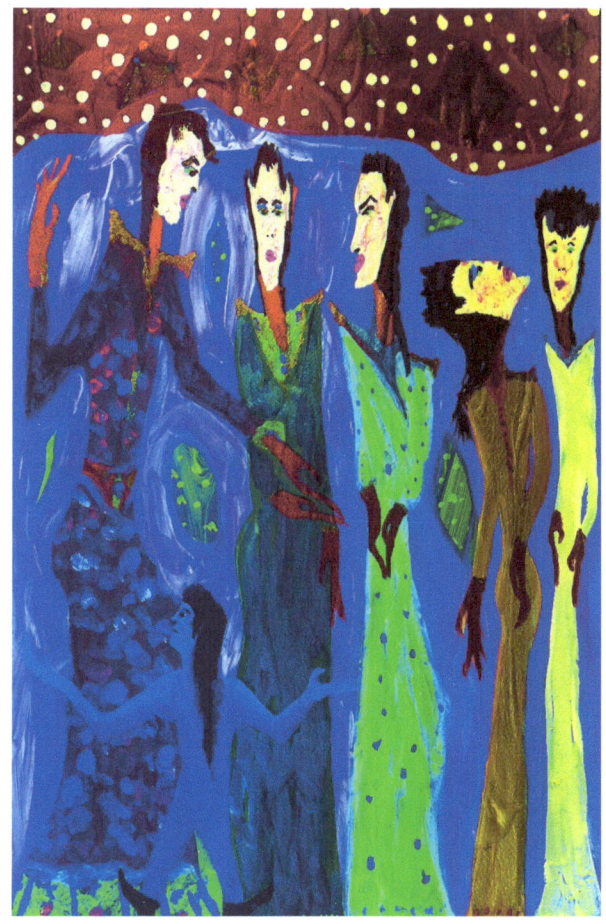

heat coming from the peculiar flames. However, there was a curious sensation…like pins and needles to the skin.

"We are in deliberation and examining the possible consequences for humanos. For their time is near." Melbo stirred a liquid into the flames which turned their color to rose and violet.

"I'm Thesuse, and my comrades of mystery are Melbo, Helba, Pythor, and Quizica. We realize the state of dual-consciousness has reached a maximus. It's either unify or die. Although, if you look at quantum fisica there can be no death just changing from one form to the other…"

"But so messy! I mean we've sent them every possible clue to get on with it. The Ascensia Gates are about to open. And I don't think the fanaticos will be necessarily the first to rise up to the vibrational state…", stated Quizica.

"The time travelin' strings are too small to fit their egos," laughed Pythor!

"Oh, if they'd just learned self-governance, it could have gone a bit more gently," exclaimed Helba. "What do you say, wizard jaguar?"

This was a tough audience. Lola waited and then spoke, "I do think there's an effect. On the planeta, they sometimes play a game called, dominHoes. Like the falling blocks, when you tip one the others fall over as well. Therefore, I think as more of them come into their truth and remember who they are, their mission as starseeders will activate matter to vibrate so fast and sweep them all into a wormhole and up they will go into 5-D!" However, in truth, Lola wanted to goad the others towards a more positive conclusion than de-evolution. There was enough apathy and depression out there in the 3-D.

"Well, perhaps. Perhaps. They will change their current state of turmoil. It's been done before. Are you aware of the codes," asked Helba?

"Maybe? Patternas? I did learn some things from Creestolatl the Grid Geomanizer," said Lola.

"Well then let's dive in and do some congurin-," proclaimed Thesuse.

*T*ogether, they trailed deeper into the cave. Tunnel after tunnel, it seemed endless. At last they reached a cavern of glowing blue stone.

"The universe of the ALL is composed of patterns. It's how the humanos recognize something and repetition brings remembrance. Right now, we are underneath the holy Mountain of Merutua. These stones reflect the lake's essence. I'd like to begin by summoning the choirs of Venera. Love, beauty, compassion, worthiness. This is the cauldron of humaniTea." Quizica sketched a sygil on the wall with a pink stone.

"Well then, I'll go next. Here I place the Vesica Pisces, the sacred womb from which all things come, the holy feminina. We birth a new egg of life for humanos to transcend," avowed Helba.

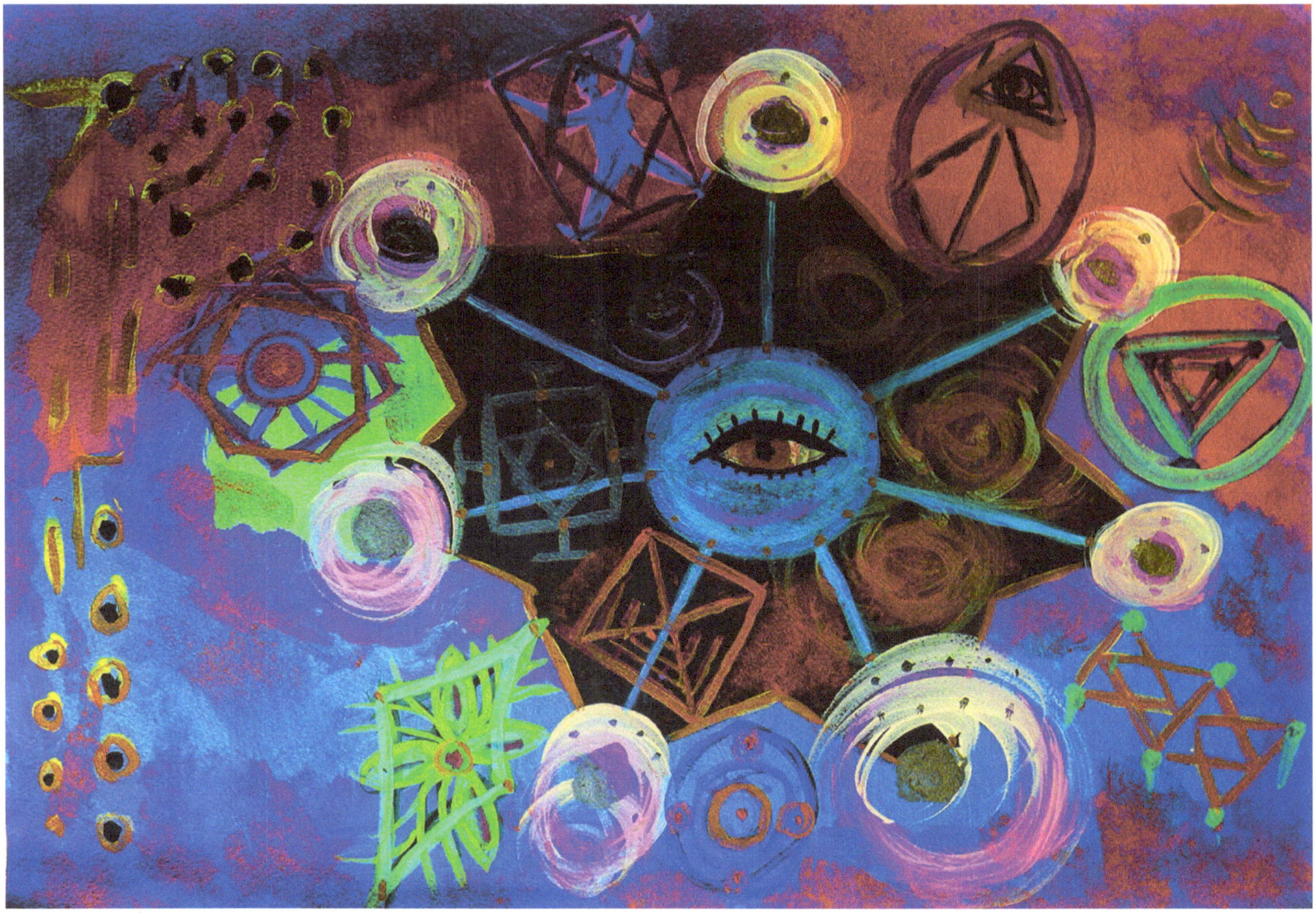

"To help solidify our intentions, I scribe this Metatron cube. Bring forward the elementals, the platonics and join them in a universal union of eloquence," declared Melbo.

Pythor picked up a purple stone and sketched a series of triangles. "Here, the flower of life blooms with all its infinite possibilities, may the pendulum swing in favor for the numerous races on the Planet of Great Consciousness."

"The spiral. Limitless inward and outward into the breath of the ALL Spin this tale into the great cycles of those that have previously mastered ascensia and wish to guide humanos on their ardent journey," added Thesuse.

They looked at Lola and waited. Lola drew a large circle and circles with in those circles. "From that which all comes, it returns. The ALL. Let this magic benefit all beings in all realms."

Then from the inside one of the circles materialized the All-Seeing-All-Knowing Eye. "It is done! It is done! It is already done!"

The hairOfants escorted Lola to the entrance and waved goodbye.

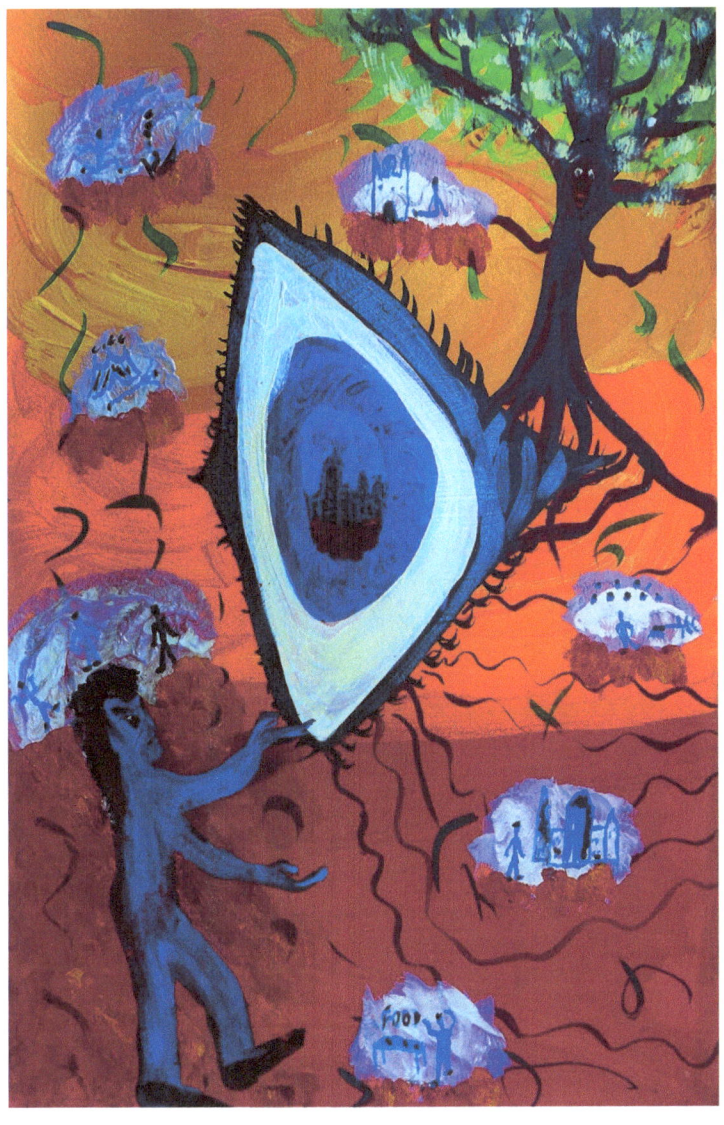

*L*ola felt magically charged up. The Lake. The cirKuss. The hairOfants. Now what? Lola turned around and the All-Seeing-All-Knowing-Eye was looking directly at Lola.

"Lola. One vision becomes another vision becomes a reality and another dissolves. Look around you. What do you see?"

Several clouds floated around Lola. Each held an image.

"These are your memories. You may call upon them as you need or transmute their energy into something else. Change the stories. Do not delude. Do not lie. Transcend. Transmute. Transform." The Eye chanted to Lola over and over as the imagery spun around heshe.

Lola watched as dancers appeared by the fire. Then the House of Many Selves. The rest A Rant. The church. And the misery of the deforestation. "Transcend. Transmute. Transform." Lola chanted those three words over and over. And soon, the images became a green forest. A market with healthy foods. And so forth…

Afterwards, the iris of the All-Seeing-All-Knowing-Eye unspiraled itself and Lola stepped inside the black hole and returned to the urban jungle.

*T*hat night, Lola had a dream. In the dream heshe encountered the many-self known as, 'ThemsNTheys'. Over and over, it became clear on how important it was to shift masks and thoughts in order to stay focused on Gaia and to calm the mind.

"Remember, you can utilize these mascaras like camouflage. Select any you wish to engage others on the planeta with care. Some will open doors, some will attract danger… Some may stir up dormant energies. Also, one could possibly absorb another's mask just by being near them… a type of osmosis for assimilation of mindsets."

Thems and theys

These and those

This and that

Which, what and why?

Many selves

For many shelves

Of whom am I!

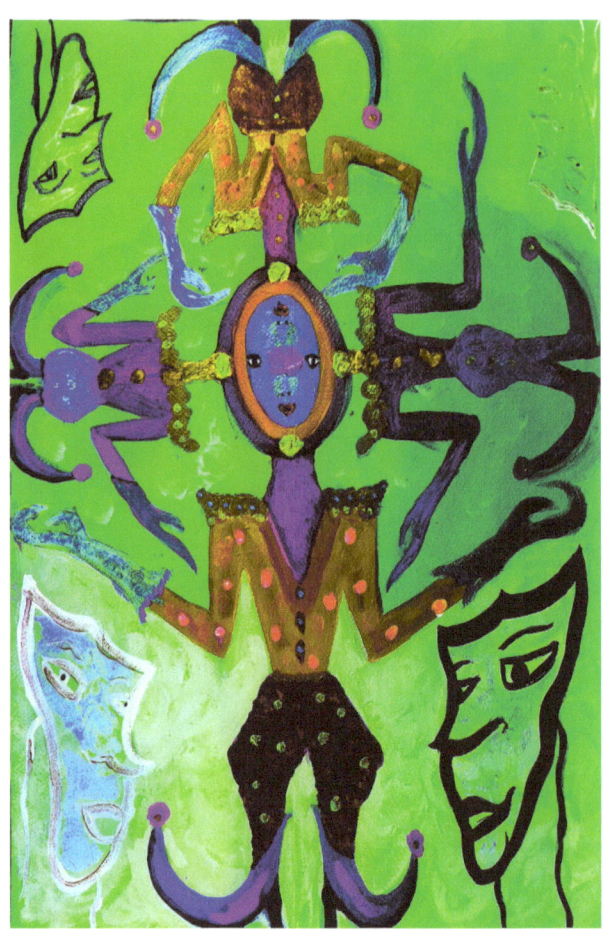

*A*t this point, Lola was wandering between worlds. One moment in 3-D, the next 5-D and other planes of consciousness as well. It seemed effortless to Lola, yet at times, it was a bit challenging to say the least. Now, after a fierce reminder from ThemsNTheys, Lola slipped into the 'doubt matrix'. Lola remembered heshe's challenging time in the magia negra grid confronting the Mask of Futility, and in doing so it had invoked a resonance of skepticism about whether humanos could collectively transcend dimensions.

Lola stood before a complex mesh filled with negative thoughts. These may or may not be mind, remembered Lola, however, with so many humanos in a state of fear with adverse gargoylas everywhere on the loose, it was ever more important to stay in a place of detachment. Even when they were at the radFae sanctuario, Lola experienced a plethora of jealousy, narcicismo, entitlement and complaisant behaviors which created a density of undesirable energy. Whether they knew of it or not, Lola was consistently focusing on harmonizing their thoughts in order to counter balance the malicious behaviors.

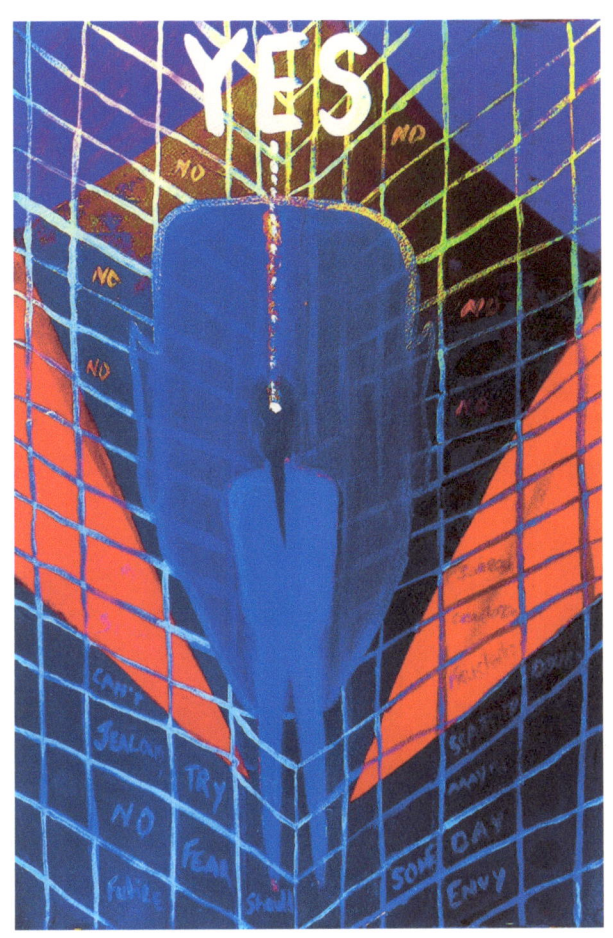

While scrutinizing their thoughts, Lola wanted to review areas of attractors. *Someday* I will. I can't. I'll try. It's futile. Denial. Doom. Wow, thought Lola, things were starting to discourage heshe a bit, even with activated shields of exuberance. It was a wonder anyone could invoke encouragement on the planeta. But, many humanos were diligent. They were determined to liberate others just like Lola. One by one, humanos were coming out in large numbers of resistance. Not so much as to resist as in fighting aggression, but more like defying effects of the delusions and control.

Lola looked around for a place to curl up and dream. Heshe walked down a narrow ally and came upon an abandoned building. Inside were a few homeless folks, they looked seemingly harmless, so Lola laid down and closed their eyes.

*T*he dream world on the Planet of Consciousness was chaotic to say the least. While dreams could be a setting for experiences to resolve unconscious problems or even time travel, at times they were also a bizarre show.

That night, Lola's dreamsphere became intertwined with the others who also slept in the room. There were innumerable negative dreams in their heads about intense backgrounds which caused them to question survival and created the mindset of scarcity. Self-esteem battles. Their inevitable acting-out had created a susceptibility which enticed entities and descarnates to attach to themselves. Perhaps without their knowing, these environments were ripe for subversive walk-in's from other areas of the universe and parallel realities.

Hence it was a rather treacherous, destabilizing night. On top of that, humanos had been seduced by and consumed horrific quantities of sabotaging white powders that stimulated brainwaves to counter balance any attempt for resolution of challenges at hand. Perhaps the usage came from a desire to escape, an attempt for a prolonged falsified euphoria, or even perverse curiosity. Unlike the plant deva elixiras, many of the refined powders were scarifying and changed the chemistry in the biofisica mass coordination of the mind—and allowed for them to be controlled that much easier by insidious leeederz.

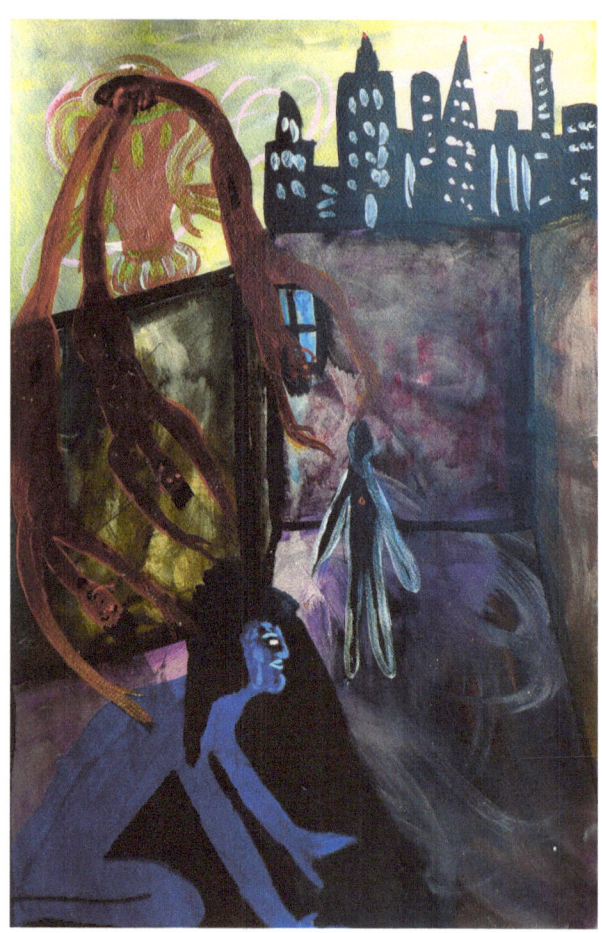

Lola was ready, and not ready. It became time for Lola to investigate what was scheming to have power over humanos ability. One thing was to reveal how to utilize shadow as opposed to discarding it or fearing it. Their mythos suggested a venture into darkness was frightening and could expose one to deathing. There were many things to consider. There were beings who distracted the healthy evolushun on the Planet of Great Consciousness and jaguar magicians needed to comprehend these energies and learn how to transmute them.

All of a sudden, the room got extremely chilly. Lola rose up to a crouching position. Something lurked in the shadows. There were energy stalkers present in the room. These forms used the most vulnerable to *walk-ins* who possessed them and used them as a vessel for increased violence.

"You! Energy trackers from other worlds, why do you attach to humanos and imprison them for your needs? What do you gain?" Lola scanned the dark space. With heshe's night vision, they saw three creatures hovering over the sleeping homoless.

"Weeee only dooo sooo when they invite usss in with their pessimistic, disparaging chargesss. Weeee feeeel thissss. There isss muuuuch you muuussst learnnn of karmic debrisss and resssolutionsssss of the epochsss of time. Iffff humanosss evolve asss isss presssumed you dessssire…weeee have no other meanssss to releassee tortoroussss karmasss for passst warsss and dessstruccction. Humano ah Day eN A hassss been modified …in mosssst. They are genetica vessicas where much can be fed upon, studied, or… perhapsss resssolved. Tonight, we mean no real harmmmm."

"I am Apathia, and the others are Ambivilotta and Delusionata. We come from galaxias far, far away. If they choose to release us? We go away. Simple."

"If you have been tortured yourself, and remember this through life-times, why is it so that you continue this chain of consciousness? How does it serve? The ALL. The greater good," asked Lola?

"Ah hah! You judge the ALL? Everything is a part of the perfection. The mastery of the essence the journey of knowing thyself. Do you fear usss? Lolaaaaa," asked Delusionata?

"I do not. I only inquire so as to guide others who wish to break free from the collapse, the entropic limits of 3-D. This is a crazy perpetual cycle of duality which has dangerously distanced itself from polarity. It seems you feed on the innocent, or instability of humanos—during an important, cathartic moment in their universal shift. This dominance is contrary to my understanding of good will. Do you wish these beings well, when you torment them so?" Lola probed them for answers. Heshe wanted to dive deep into this stance on incongruent forms and their obliviousness to dishonor.

"In some respect. We need them. They consume animals. They consume and pollute their air and water with material greed. We need their elements. If too many evolve we need to create another realm. That takes millennia," shared Apathia.

"This story you weave, here and now, conspiracy or truth?" Lola peered at the skyskrapers which menacingly loomed as far as heshe could see—a complete abandonment of the natura source, the aesthetica of trees, tranimals…

"Then, I ask you to immediately leave these homoless and rest yourselves. I now see that the complexity is expansive. Those that desire then, will be released from your influence and this doubt matrix. Be gone." Lola whispered sternly to the gargolas.

Ambivilotta stubbornly refused to leave. The gargola shapeshifted into Morgano while Lola slept. Ambivilotta entered Lola's dreamsphere penetrating heshe's shields… a violation of agreements to non-intervention. In the dreamsphere the entity changed into Lola's divine twin, Morgano. This was spawned in order to represent Lola's desire for a twin flame or divine twin.

"This is the feeling they have. Take this! You pompous arrogant faggot faux wizard! BETRAYAL! They have felt the lecherous fangs of blood riddled deceitfulness. You stroll this planet with arrogance and aloofness. Yet their sadness is defiled with distrust of energies from avatarian questers such as yourself!" Ambivilotta, as Morgano, violently punched through Lola's heart space. Lola flung against the wall. Heshe was thrown into complete emptiness and confusion. Shocked. Gasping for air. Torn inside.

"This is how they feel! They have seen so much pain, destruction, violence, torture and you come

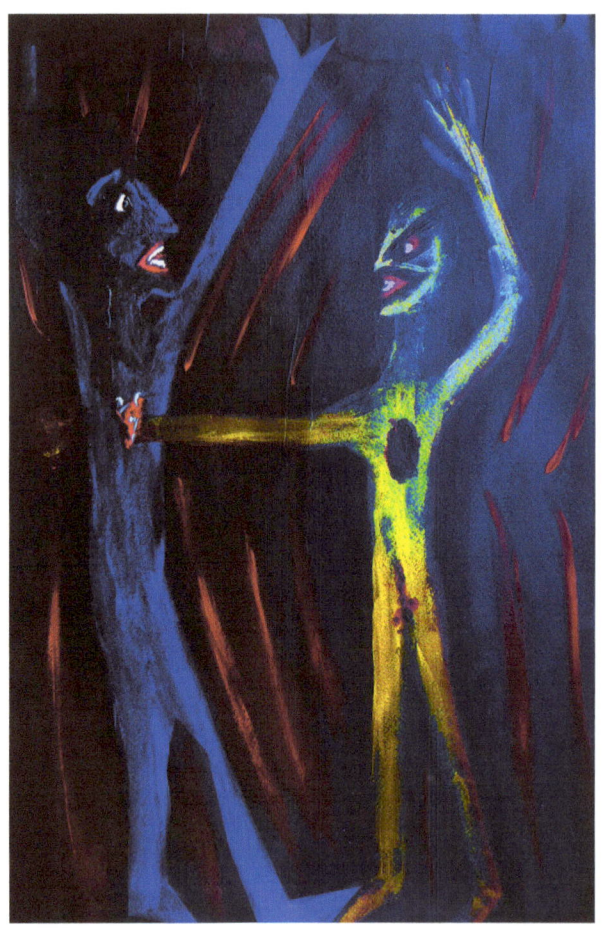

here wondering why we feed off it?! At least we invigorate and expose its ugly truth. You seem to deny it—at the very least, refuse it exists as some unworthy aspect of the ALL. Truth be known, yes, they can disallow these reactions for causations and fates that engulf the universes and the 3-D realms with terror. Yet, you reek of the bourgeois gurus on the planeta! Even though they activated higher laws in attempt to integrate sacred laws of consciousness they have failed humanos," shouted Ambivilotta!

"Please why do you do this to me?" Lola choked. Heshe's lungs struggled and took strenuous gasps. "Your constructs have no depth. These beings have a right to be vengeful, even full of rage! We lift their malevolence to a place of resolve that you have yet to understand."

Lola saw that the heartspace was actually empty and that it was not Morgano at all, but an entity. Lola began to hum and sing a song in order to reharmonize the situation. This would neutralize the extremeness of the action.

"I hear you. I will consider what you have shared. I have been shielded from the deepest pains of their societies and their lengthy periods of development. You are released." Lola stood up, pushed the door open and walked out into the hallway.

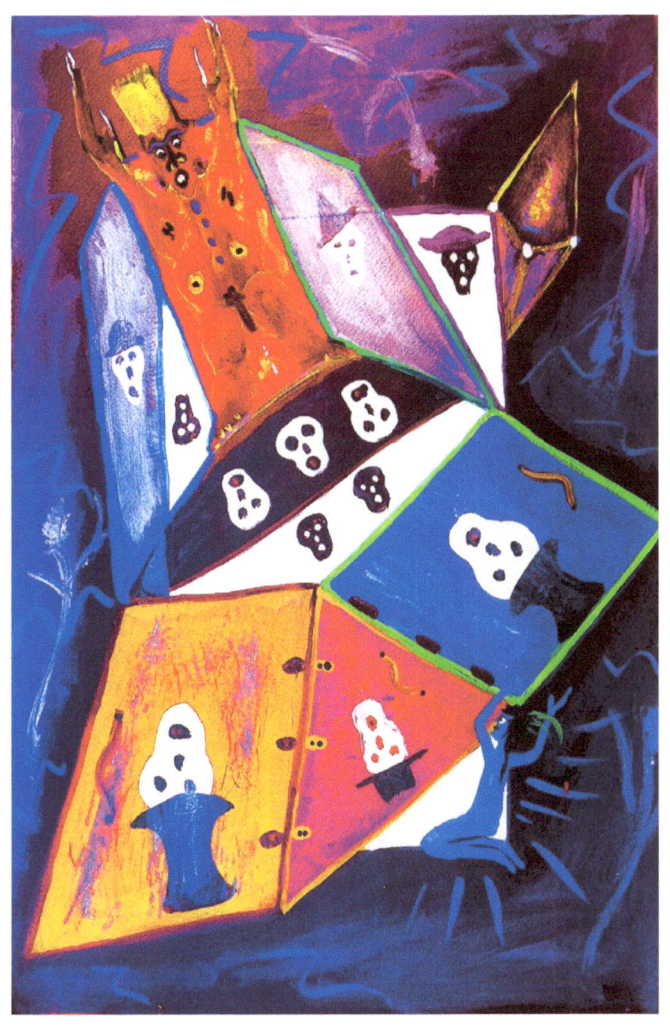

A few steps away heshe saw a stairway. Lola descended the staircase while it metamorphosed into a tunnel and plunged heshe into a dark chamber. Shaking the dust from their hair, Lola glanced around the room. The space was filled with doors, windows and mirrors.

Cackling sounds of hilarity were heard coming from behind a large grey door. Boom! A wall splintered into fragments and shattered across the floor. An enormous fiery red creature with an orange and green Mohawk charged into the center of the chamber. Skeletal heads materialized in mirrors and hysterically laughed. More skulls peered from behind doors.

"Welcome to the Underwareworld gurrrrrl. Or themthosethey up there may call it the more reserved term, the Underworld… or I rather like the word, Hell. Hot n spicy inferno. Place of the damned—I'll be damned!" The furious red being stormed toward Lola and spat onto the floor. Spittle flew from its mouth with each word as it shouted. "Well then, let's get to the introduction junctions. I'm Trickeey Rageina, Queen of Guiles! A distant relation to your old buddies, Jaguar Queen Diva and Jaguar Serpiente. You do remember them don't you little jaguar?"

Lola tried to speak, but was interrupted.

"Well I'm here to tell you a bitter truth about humanos and why they're still in that shit world… lalala."

"Of course, I remember those two, but they weren't as threatening as you," scowled Lola.

"Well scuuuuuuuuuzzzz me." Trickeey took a mocking bow. "I pose no threat. Though I do reveal. Some refer to me as the shadow mirror. I can't get why they wanna avoid lessons from the netherworlds…

if they only knew that by ignoring this vital part of the dual I tea, they activate demonias… you know… the one's in their story books. You saw 'em… their caricatures from Holy-Wood cinemamas and lawd knows those religi-osos and their seditious govern'ners, selected leeederz. OMG. It's a mess gurrrll. I'm not here to hurt you." Trickeey reached out to pet Lola. "Nice jaguar."

"Then what is it you wish for them or maybe even for me to learn? Perhaps with a worthy definition or lessons I could reveal things to them better," chimed Lola.

"Sure kid. I can do that. Sit a spell." Trickeey motioned some of the skeletals to her side. "Well first off, many of them choose a life of false desire, rather than from the heart. They think that life is all purity, with no bumps or farts. Misery, anxiety… jeeebus me, they love depression… and all them RXXX-pills for their ongoing, unchecked dilemmas. Woe is me. A bunch of worthless addicts. Shit they do live in hell. This is paradise compared to theirs. No delusionata here!

Secondly, all that hoarding. Money! Money! Money! Fame! They lussst for it! Yeah, I guess those that have a shit ton of things may be thinking they can influence the outcome of their journey with them, but in the end, they all die… That's the contract. Well? Back to 0. Nothing. Back onto the karmic freeway. You can't take all that stuff from the palace, Alice, *everyone* ends up underneath a hard tombstone. Ask the Egypshuns! Bahahahahah!"

"I think some of them get that. Impermanence. But what else," asked Lola?

"Jeez. We just want 'em to come down and have a drink with us. Chill the frick out. They arrive here mostly to rebalance the elemental aspects. Some of 'em have too much wind, and I don't mean from eatin' beans, and then what remains is the elements of water or fire and neither of those is too good on their own." Trickeeey pulled a skeletal onto her lap. "Jeez, you look like you seen it all before dude. Why don't you share a lesson or two with us?"

The Skeletal rattled and adjusted its bones into a standing position. "I decree that life is short. Enjoy what you have—all of it. It keeps changing. Open up to the possibility. Change is a seed of wisdom. Don't fear death, instead relish in the small ones each day. Treat the body with reverence, drink better champagne!"

The Skeletal seemed rather amused by its joke. "Transform anger into vigorous energy to feel change. Embrace the disturbances. OK, so you fell off the bike and it hurt. Afterwards you go to the repair shop and get it fixed. While there... you met a good f---k or your lover. Right? Synchronic bubonic tonic!" The skeletal snickered.

"Sure, rebirth is a process but it seems like so many are getting weary from prolonged pain," added Lola.

"Honestly, what they hunger for is here with us…in the shadows. Engage both the positive and the negative." Trickeey started to do a jig. "All that sufferin' and strife, yeah it sucks to the max, but let 'em know, find a way to ground, cuz those depressions—don't get addicted to them or hang on to 'em like a favorite toy—they are the device to help 'em with a richer, more—key word—*conscious* life. Look, seeking truth by avoiding risks or challenges is just gonna make the fall into this place that much more difficult. At first it may taste bitter, but the more you do it the better you get at it and soon it'll taste like a piece o' candy. That Mixtress YUM would like that… Hey, I'm promoting dental decay!"

"It seems like so many are immersed in blame or guilt—even frozen in apathy to point they have normalized tragedy. And I don't mean the kind of tragedy that you see on arrival here," stated Lola.

"Yeah, I hear it's pretty intense up there now. I think you outta go see my friend Polarina before you head up to the light of day. She can share more on the magic of refining duality. In any case… remind those humanos it's about the journey not the destination."

Lola felt the floor rise up very quickly. They watched as Trickeey and the skeletals were left below.

*O*nce the floor had stopped moving, Lola saw a door at the end of the room. By now, Lola was used to multiple dimensions, universos and parallel twirlds, but were Humanos aware of them? I'm sure they exist in their perception. Soon it would be time to inform more of them about the transition and tools for guidance.

Heshe opened the door. It was beautiful inside. It smelled like roses. There was a large formation of arrows from floor to ceiling in the middle of the room. Lola heard someone walking down a corridor.

"Dear Lola! I've heard of you through the ethers… so good of you to join our magic here on the 3rd-dimensiona." Polarina smiled. "My dear wonder-being, are you aware of the mass opposition on the planeta and its seemingly endless 'stuckness'? Alas, they seemed obsessed, or maybe captivated by peculiar manifestations of dual I tea. Right and wrong. Up and down. This and that. Trickeey was right. Well, anyway, let me see if I can explain it a different way through the elementals."

Polarina handed two masks for Lola to reference. "3-D of course has two opposing energies. Thus duality. Those two energies split into four—mind, body, soul and spirit. Right now, Gaia's realm has a

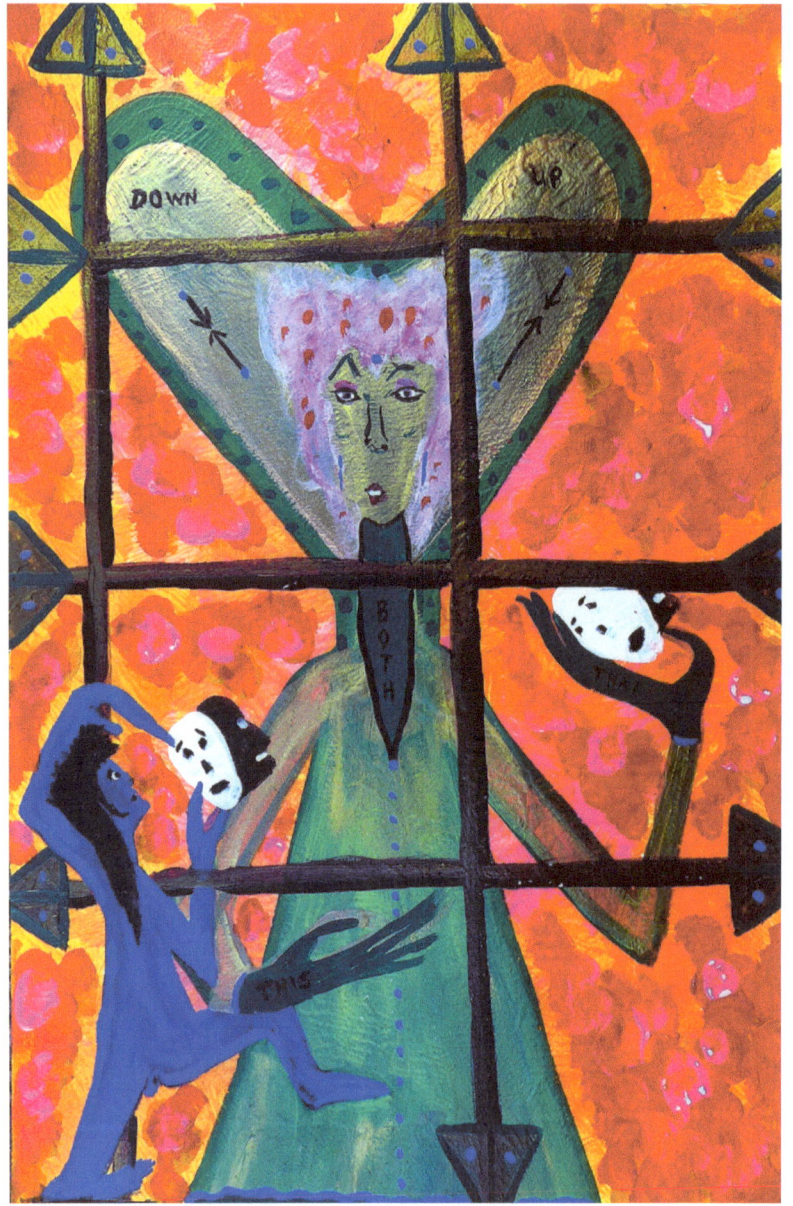

dominance of Air/Mind. Hence, when that gets burnt out or displaced, water comes into action often unbalanced as well, for it has not been tended. It shows up as depression or sadness. In general, if one of the elements is out of balance, it magnetizes what it needs to be tended to, or heard. Ultimately these places of instability are the soul asking to be heard and inner work to be cultivated. Please share with them that it is important not to conceal feelings or one risks too much fiery energy, and that often results in a trip to the UnderwareWorld of Trickeey. Often, they may not have to go to such extremes. Furthermore, their trip to the UnderWorld may be for the collective. They g there for the group soul to gather wisdom and mirror that wisdom into the shared sphere. Does this help you understand, Lola?"

"Immeasurably. Thank you so much." Lola was beamed with joy.

"Sometimes, the opposition has a desire to actually magnetize what they want or need. Hence if intended, they direct the magic of, I would like to invite in… then it becomes harmonic polarity. Like the poles of the planeta in union. Quite a paradox box no? The density is born from conflict, heterogeneous energy.

However, the resolve for your lovely jaguar magicians and their friends, is to bring dual consciousness into oneness through homogeneous harmonized energy. Then the hemisfericas of the cerebros, or brains can be bridged and an entirely new level of consciousness be birthed.

This may be why the two-spirit, qweer, and multi-genders are considered a threat. There are those that fear losing control of the tension in dual consciousness and prefer to continue hypnotizing them with fear." Polarina grabbed another mask that looked like it had blood dripping from it.

"Anyway, to continue, be wizened of the many that have profited from the raging battles and whose hearts have turned to stone. The wars. The dis-ease. False prophet-fits." Polarina pointed to the sky. "Look, here comes SwanSong! Yes, yes. Fly onwards, now with the grace, eloquence and kindness of 5-D. Channel that into everyone you contact. This could very well help the status of change on the planeta. Fair thee well lovely Lola…"

Polarina waved as Lola flew off into the sky with SwanSong.

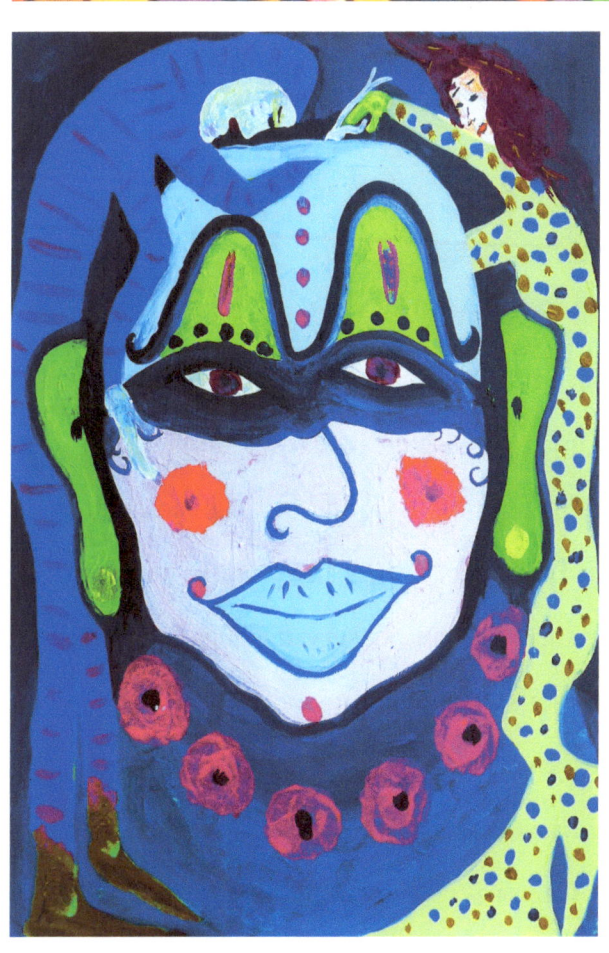

Lola was gently released by SwanSong in front of a small tent in the forest. While Lola had acquired profound knowledge, heshe felt a strong pang of sorrow. Heshe felt remorse for perhaps not having done enough for humanos.

"Hey you! Come over here! I've come here to chew bubble gum and kiss ass! I'm Hey-Okey!"

Yet another Klown. This one was quite large and round and reminded Lola of Payaso Pyneal. Heshe loved the Klowns. Two figures lamented above Hey-Okey.

"Yeah, Lola. I get it. Honey, sorrow is just the flip side of joy. World view can sometimes be atrocious. Really! The nerve. Sadness has veiled entire regions. I've tried different make-up, wigs, even our friend the pink elefant but it's hard for them to see a way out of their emotional filterin." Hey-Okey shook off the Lamentors.

"You know joy medicine? Not the bullshit patronizing crap—it gets better—blah blah. I mean, joy that wiggles a crack in the doom blooms. Using the opposite sides of the coins to spin a new illusion, magnetize 'em to it." Hey Okey danced. "It's the Klown in me, I guess. Fun. Fun. Fun. But, fun that doesn't hurt others."

"Honestly, I do feel sad, Hey-Okey. Yeah, I know this spell of emotivas, I've been cautioned of its weight and dominance," shared Lola.

"Hey, do you understand compersion? Finding joy in another's joy and NOT feeling jealous of it, just immersing yourself in it like a warm bath with chocolate cake and some good music and maybe some flowers, candles, um a velvet robe, a hookah full of weeder… you get my point? Be in the glow of the possibility. Feel it. Dance it. Sing it. Climb up on it. Dive into it. The humanos sit in front of their consistent rattlingbox of the TeeVee—sheesh the projections. Oh Lola, look at me, travel with my joy. I mean it's not wrong to feel sad, of course, there's the sad Klown, my cousin, Depreshonterwootertooter… but let those emotivas fly away like balloons… ya don't want any of them nasty entity creeps buggin' you out."

"Thanks, Hey-Okey, I feel better already. I'm gonna go look for some of my friends. See ya." Lola took off into the forest.

*I*t was a crisp, gorgeous dawn. It seemed like a considerable amount of time had passed since the interval with the radFae at the sanctuario. Lola wanted to reconnect with Marvavilla and discuss ways to invite jaguar magicians and their allies into a deeper connection. It was time to invoke creative resolutions and resolve harmonic energies for the Planet of Great Consciousness. Lola went off to wander through a vast field. They saw a bright, flamboyant building on the horizon. Heshe heard trumpets blaring and glorious laughter.

When approaching the amazing structure, Lola stopped for a moment and observed a huge limozene drive up to the front doors. The window went down and a familiar crimson being popped their head out.

"Heeeeeeyyyyy you made it back from the humano underwareworld! It's me Calusaris! What's up? Can you believe this? Look at this crapper! Eveeel lurks. Profiteers have mask-marketed the cirKuss. Ah well. Wanna go inside with me and see if we can shake it up a bit? Eh?" Calusaris jumped out of the vehiculo and raced towards the door. He motioned for Lola to join him.

Suddenly, a Klown jumped off the roof of the building and plopped directly in front of Lola.

The Klown let out an enormous fart-like sound that blasted from their lips. "Hmph! Well I'll say. These idiotas fired all the Klowns? The boss, EgoMania, says that we cost 'em too much and folks only wanna see the lights and hear the music and eat more and more shooogar. Well, I'll see about that! You all going

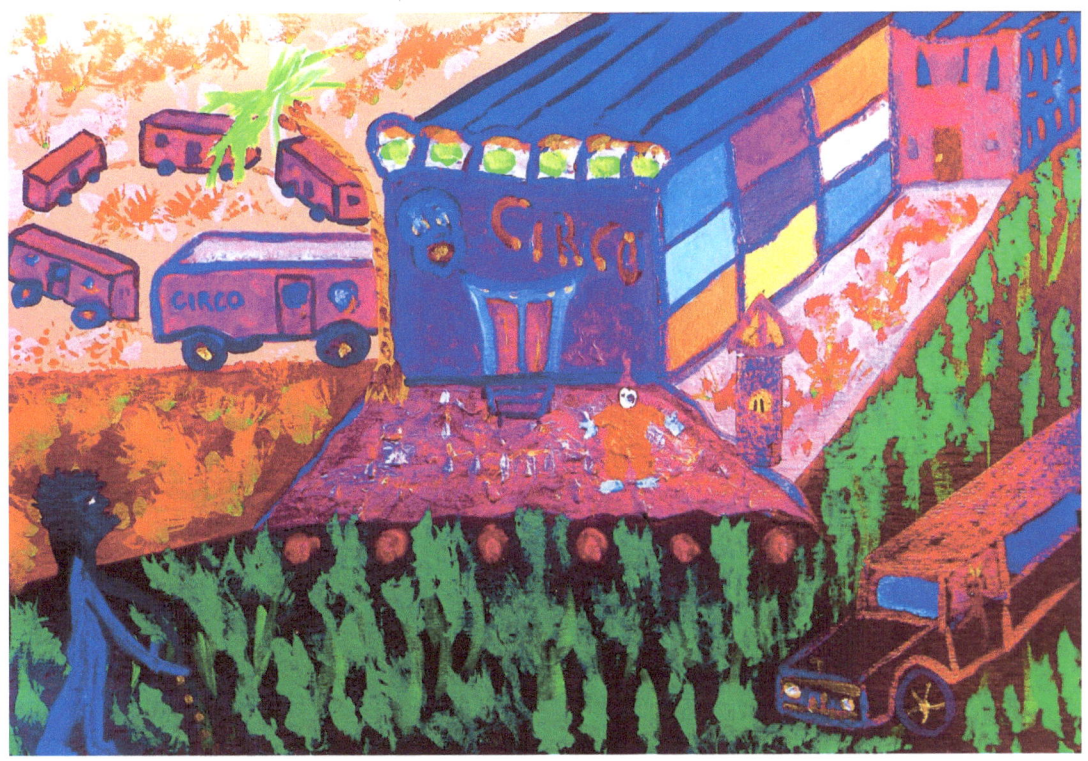

in? Let me join you. Shhh… Secretly, in one of those caravans over there are a hundred or so other Klowns stuffed inside like sardinas!"

The three of them marched inside without bothering to buy a ticket. Once inside, the cirKuss the energy seemed rather subdued. No one in the audience was smiling. Their eyes were empty and cold.

"Ok. Klown-klown, do you have a plan? This place is depressing to say the least. Look at them! All hypnotized by the drivel of wealth and fame. No spirit." Calusaris poked a few of the viewers who didn't seem to notice or feel anything.

"I'll run out and get 'em all lined up by the doors. You and Lola get as close to the stage as possible. Once we are inside let's take over this dead cirKuss and give them a surprise pirate piñata style bombastic woovoo carn-e-Val, what do you say?" Klown ran outside to get the other jesters.

Lola watched as lifeless acrobaticos swung limply from the trapeze. Heshe was fearful of them falling for it seemed they too were in a deep depression, almost wanting to fall to their deaths. Something must be done!

Calusaris motioned to Lola from a hidden area next to the stage. "Come on, we'll wait here for the big-bang surprise of Klown lunacy. You know... it's the full moon tonight. Yeee hawwww!"

Boom! Bang! Whoa! Trumpets. Cymbals. Xylophones. Accordiones, every instrument blasted onto stage with literally hundreds of Klowns. Colors and smiles exploded onto stage. The audience jolted from somnambulant states and gazed suspiciously upon the Klown piratas.

"We are the thunderbird and the trickster! Leave these bloody footprints of money and orthodoxy beyond and join us in our crazy wisdom!" Bam! Cymbals crashed. A trumpeter tooted for jugglers to come onto stage. Fake paper money fell from the ceiling causing a brief pandemonium until the audience discovered the illusion. Balloons exploded that were filled with laughing gas.

Lola and Calusaris went to the emcees and biznessmeanies who owned the show. They ripped off their masks and revealed demonias behind them. "Who are these gangsterz that you bow down to? Who do you want controlling your every move while they destroy the vital life force of the Planet of Great Consciousness?" Calusaris jumped up and down cutting strings that held viewers in a trance.

Calusaris fed laughing gas to some of the leederz in their privileged box seats. Once they got a whiff of it, the leeederz stripped down naked and jumped onto stage. Then they danced like the buffoons they were. The audience roared with laughter.

"It's time to change," shouted a Klown! Immediately, hundreds of Klowns did a revealing strip change and each of them turned vibrant blue! Then purple! Then orange! All the colors of the rainbow!

"What? Have we all gone spiritually dumb? Or numb? Why ya'll so glum? Good lawd give 'em some gum," shouted a Klown! Moments later a basket swung above the audience and spilled mountains of bubble gum. The audience, to their delight, began chewing and blowing bubbles. They popped their mouthfulls of goo and exploded onto each other's face.

Lola looked beyond the chaos and saw Marvavilla waved to heshe. Heshe darted across the floor. "Heeeeyyy! Can you believe this? We took over the show!"

"Love it. Come with me. These tricksters are doing a great job. Im going to show you another theatre,

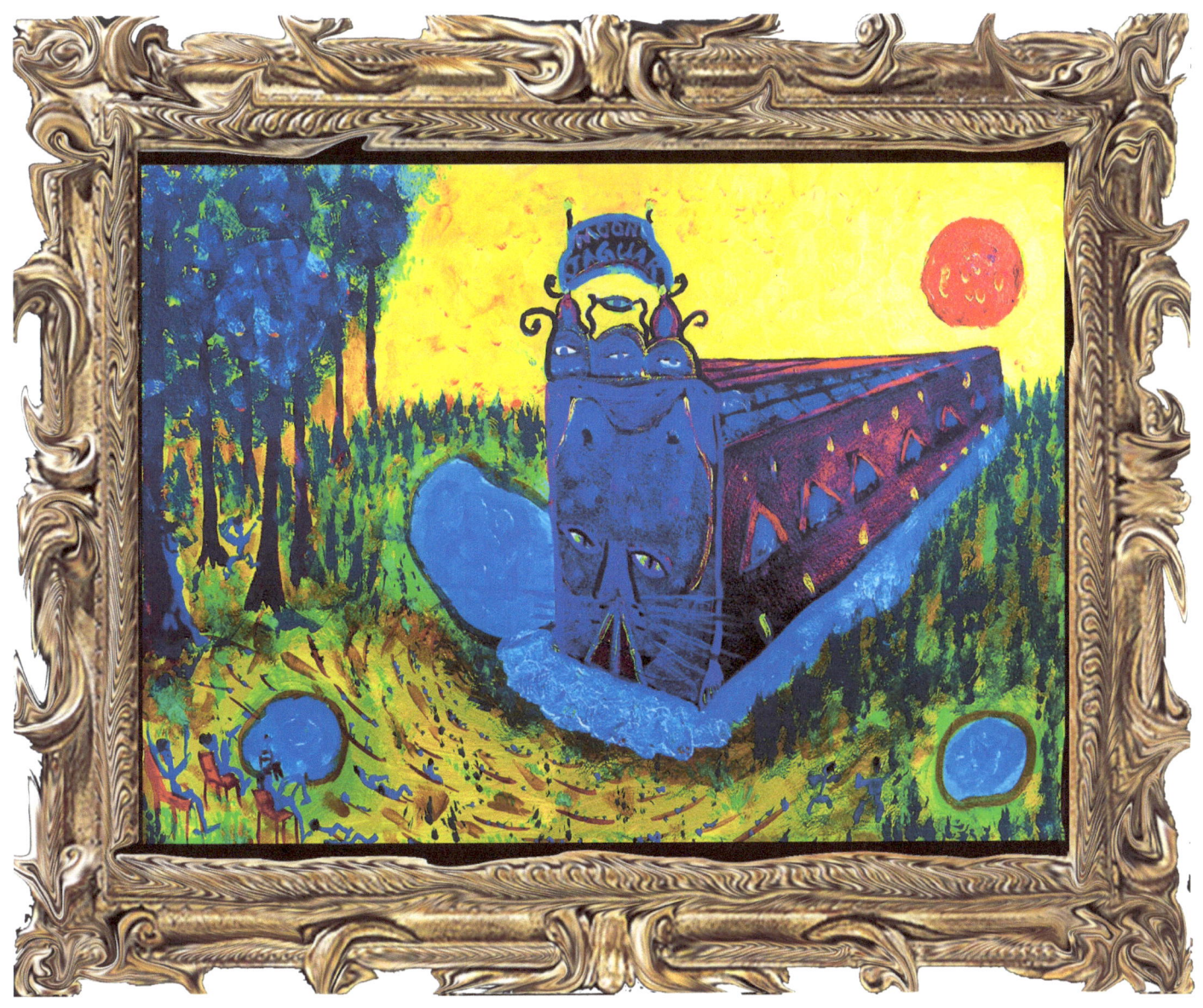

called the Moon Jaguar. It's deeper in the woods and illumined only on full moons. We better get there soon." Lola and Marvavilla escaped the silly madness and darted into the forest.

"Not all humanos are addicted to that malarkey. Like I said in the past, a whole lotta folks are wakin' up on the planeta. These are the one's you wanna reach out to, known as the awakeners'. Let's give 'em a little boost." Marvavilla smiled and took Lola's hand.

They walked into a vast ravine. A large meadow spread before them like an outdoor amphitheater. There was a large gold, purple and iridescent blue building in the middle of a lake. The moon and sun illuminated the structure. How was all this possible, Lola wondered? Heshe's excitement vibrated through every bone.

It seemed Marvavilla knew everyone. They meandered through the seating and approached the lagoon which surrounded the giant theatre. It was glorious to behold. Everyone was glowing in bliss.

"Lola, you should perform here!" Marvavilla pointed to the stage entrance. "I mean, just get up there and share a bit of your story. Let them hear that you have traveled from far away in order to enhance the emerging energy within us. Whatever you want. This is your time. *Our* time."

"Will you join me? I don't want it to be all about me. Yet, like you said perhaps I can offer something to the formation of the language of light and invite them to weave an event construct." Lola paused. "Oh, I know what I can do." Lola joined Marvavilla and went backstage.

"You know what's so cool about this place? Everything 'inside' can also be seen to those on the outside. There really isn't any inside of the theatre, I mean, it's hard to explain, but your story is projected through the transparent walls. Some of the techno-genies figured out how to transpose the density. Super cool, eh?" Marvavilla looked through some of the costumes and found an elegant purple velvet jacket. "You want some drag? Come on it's fun. Play with the masks. Put one on me and yourself."

"Why not?" Lola rummaged through the mounds of fabric and pulled out a green wig and emerald cape. Heshe twirled around. "How's this?"

Marvavilla came up and kissed Lola on the cheek. "I love it. The Mago Emcee has invited us to go on now!"

Lola gasped. What was heshe doing? A moment of truth. Out there were perhaps thousands of jaguar magicians and their allies. Well then, heshe would share a moment of reflection.

Smiles upon smiles greeted Lola. Marvavilla had grabbed a flute and played softly in the background as another friend beat a slow rhythmic beat.

"Greetings divine mirrors! Look around you! We are the one's we have been waiting for. The shores are crumbling. Be not afraid. Jump in the river. Flow." Whistles and cheers from the audience roared filling the forest up to the rafters of the theatre.

"This, my friends, is not about me and it's not about a stage. It is about remembering who you are and joining, unifying the possibilities." Lola paused and prayed. Oh, graces of the Phoenix and Ocelotl guide my voice. Lola continued, "I have literally time traveled to be here. From the innocence of the Selva, I bring you the wisdom of my teachers, the Jaguar Magician, Ocelotl, and the Phoenix, the magnificence of the ALL-Seeing-ALL- Knowing-Eye and many others. I feel you! This awakening has been spoken of in your wisdom teachings. The clouds of delusion break apart and reveal truth. I am of the qweer-multi-gender form. We have all come into the wholeness of gender and self-identity. We are children of the stars. Your ah-Day-eN-A is reorganizing and vibrating at such rate that this dimension no longer suits your will. I have come from another dimension, like others before, NOT to be worshiped, please not that, yet, until now, the force of change has been idling. It has certainly risen up and down over the epoch of humanos and their existence. Yet now, it quickens to a point of no return."

Lola motioned for Marvavilla to join heshe. "This is my divine twin. I have many twin flames that span ages and realities. Rest assured that each thought, each idea, each word has a resonant tone that brings a reality. So, with me, will you join me? Soon I will traverse from here and open the 13 gates of consciousness for all to follow. You may freely choose to ascend this realm with myself and many others.

It is not a cult, nor following, it is not a formed religion, the only thing one is invited to consider here is to believe in the capacity of who you are and your capability as a master. This world as you know is a projection of thought forms. The vegetated mass of a conscious individuals and the collective forum is in a period of wild reformation. My friend here, Marvavilla, comes with me from the Karn-I-Vals of transcendence. Toss away your masks and see who you are, nothing more, nothing less than the ALL. In this, you indeed have the capacity to lift Gaia and her planeta of Great Consciousness to a new vibrational realm know as Lambda. Here duality is polarity and harmonized into oneness. There will be no us or them, only love. No more fear. Only truth and trust. To do this means to completely forgive. To step into a place of non-attachment. This is something very different from ambivalence or 'not-caring'. I assure you, no one will do the ascension for you. It is your free will, your motion of thought and action that will carry you along to a higher vibration."

Just then, hundreds upon hundreds of flower kissers took over the attention in the enormous theatre.

The magnificent birds hummed their way through the forest.

There was nothing more to say. With that, Lola and Marvavilla wandered off the stage and let the flower kissers do their magic.

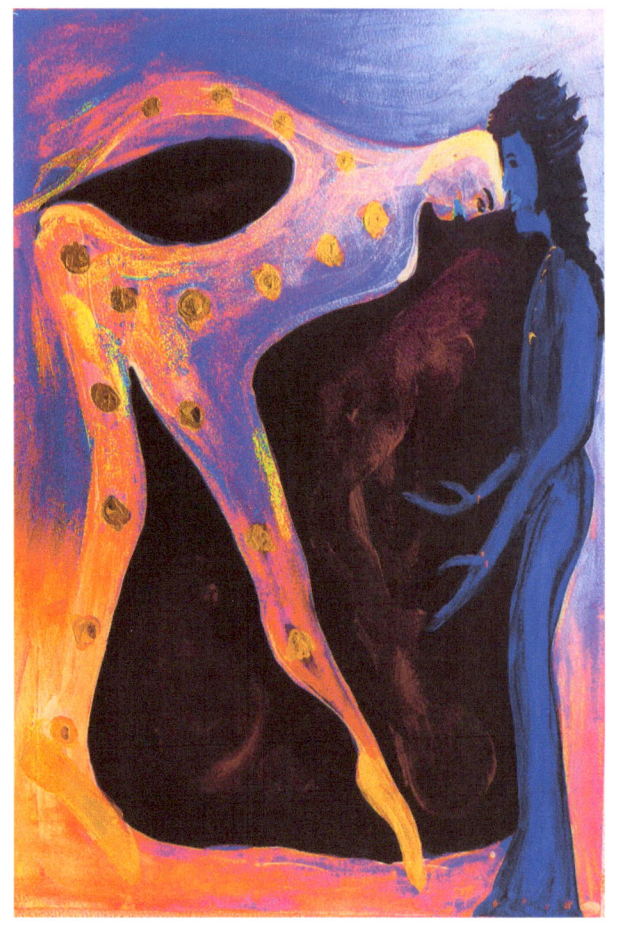

*W*hile backstage they centered their energy and restored themselves from the wild vibrations of the stage. Lola noticed a spinning danzer to their side. Twirling, floating off the floor, spinning, spiraling, like a feather in the wind.

"Whooo is that, Marvavilla," asked Lola? The danzer didn't give Marvavilla anytime to answer.

"Greetings lovely Lola! I am BailaRina Cougararee. I am spinning with the joy of your words. Our words. Thank you." The danzer bowed to Lola. "You were correct to reference this theatrical center as a place to align awakening. Indeed, as a danzer, I have learned how to detach my body from gravity." The danzer took a leap high into the air, floated a moment and landed softly on their feet.

"Wow that is so cool. I feel almost humano. I mean, I can feel the growing empathic state of their consciousness. You are a danzer. How does your movement inform them... the people out there," asked Lola?

"Wisely postulated question. Dancing helps one to uncover the dark spots of the heart. Connecting vision with foresight, to see, to move, to become free from cultural restrictions and inhibitions. It can be beyond performance. As I spin around, nothing can attach to me, blood fills my veins and my mind goes into ecstatica fields. After each of these theatrical episodes we often dance. Everyone joins us in the oneness of formation. They can focus on 5-D consciousness, the place where you are from. As they move the vibration increases, and truth flows into them. They can hear themselves. The strife of competition, poverty and menacing control, slowly, gently, slip away into space and are transformed. When one does mirror dancing such as that, they see the magic of '*in la kech*' —I am another you.

Marvavilla picked up a drum and played a hypnotic tone while others picked up flutes and rattles.

"As we dance, we also cleanse. Breath. Emotions. Connect to creativity of the moment. Through joyful fun, one infuses internally with heart medicine, heart-knowing."

"So, it is an inspiring movement. A sort of physical transformation that also clears the mind connecting them to source. How wonderful to connect them through dance to something bigger, to bliss, to step into the infinite space between, beyond their normal daily existence."

Lola began to spin and soon everyone backstage was dancing.

"*T*he Theater of Life. All the world's a stage. This Moon Jaguar Theatre is joining cycles, illusions to visions, vision to sovereignty," declared Marvavilla. They stopped playing music and walked into small village near to the citay. They enjoyed tea with BailaRina Cougaree, and a few others.

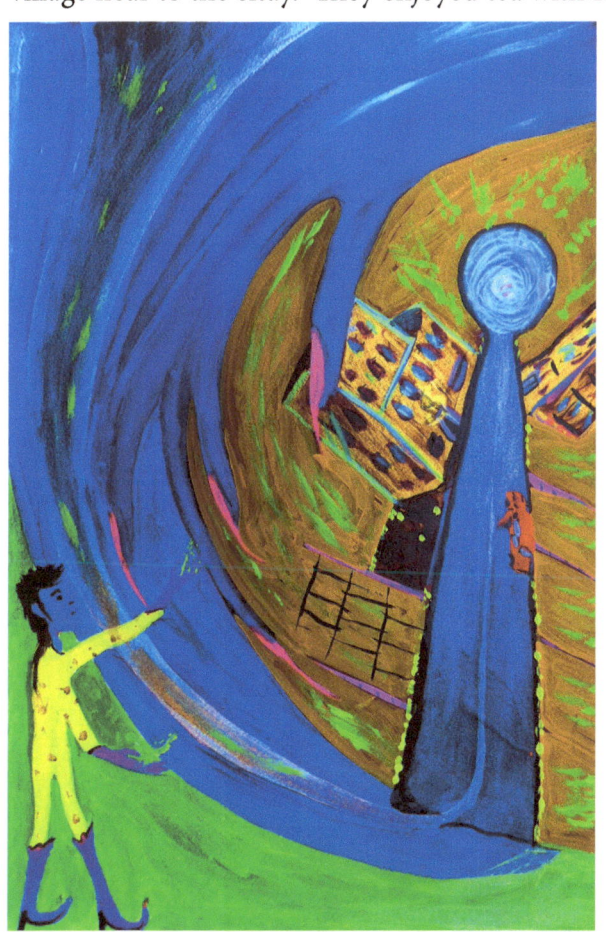

"Where to now? We can lead them, or rather invite them to walk through the portal of illumination? Will they see it in time," wondered Lola?

"Look!", Marvavilla pointed to the horizon. Thousands from the audience were parading toward the city. Something had indeed changed.

The majestic display had invigorated such energy of heart connection, that those who had been in the forest were now dancing in the streets. Singing. Lifting their hearts with joy as they passed. Humanos abandoned their cars and joined the procession.

The hand of the ALL appeared and swept through the air. As it passed the forest, the villages, and finally the citay, it stopped and suspended at the end of a boulevard. A small circle of vaporous energy swirled into motion. It grew larger and larger until it was bigger than the tallest skyscraper.

"The portal of transformation was opened. It seemed enough have focused their will for the desired dream and have now actualized the event construct to complete the transformation," stated Lola. "Let's join them. I have seen many things, but this is different. The dimensions have opened a hoya negra of infinite possibilities. Indeed, the jaguar magicians are liberating the perception on the Planet of Great Consciousness."

They grabbed others hands and wandered into the spiral.

*O*nce Lola stepped into the giant portal, heshe was separated from the others. Lola was met by Phoenix and Ocelotl. They silently approached heshe and offered a large piece of onyxia in the shape of a humano's heart.

Lola sensed this was some sort of key to open the portal for others. Heshe held up the heart-shaped stone for the Phoenix. The bird flashed into flames immediately after it took the onyxia into its beak.

"Eat this heart. Passion of desire for outcome. I offer it up to the greater wisdom and magic of the moment. The twinkling of truth that has arrived. I transfer any control I may have for a desired outcome. With all its wonder, I join myself with the higher self that is inside each humano to awaken of them to the 13 Gates of Consciousness. Thus, let fire eagle eat jaguar's heart!" Lola raised both arms into the air and

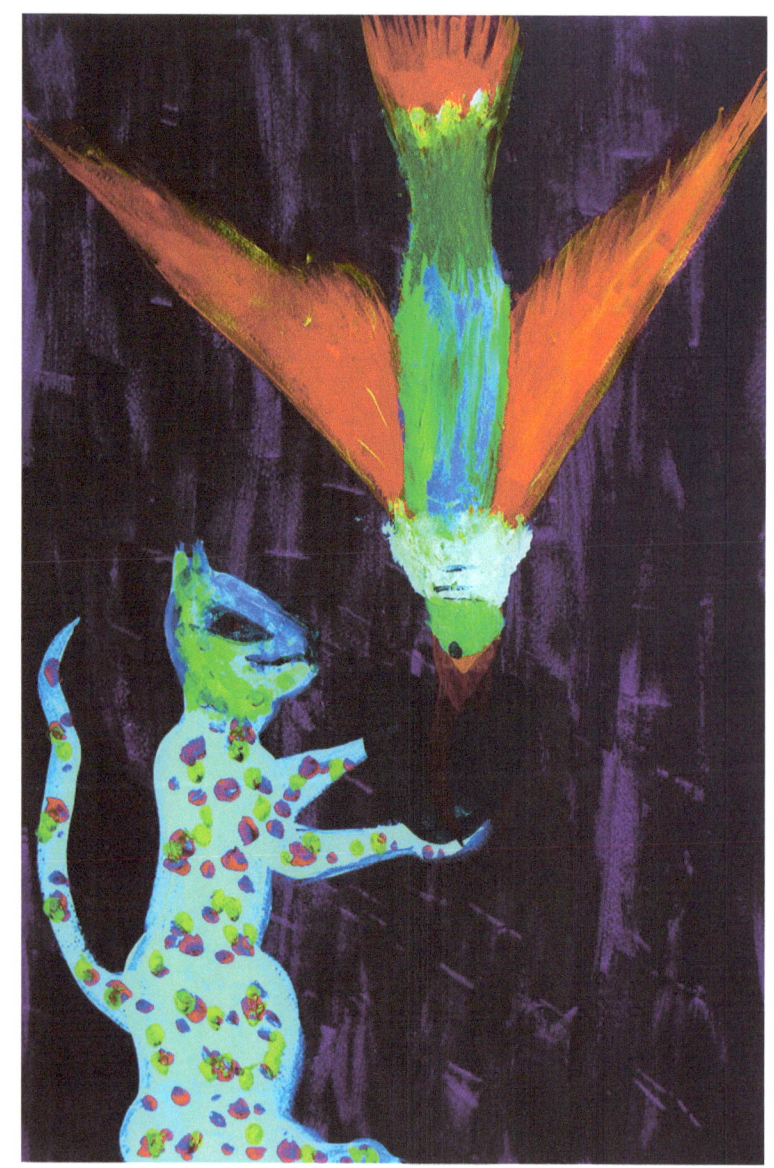

c. huilo c.

clapped three times. "It is done! It is done! It is already done!"

"Dear Lola, what wonderful magic! There are others waiting to share with you on how to weave these vibrations carefully into the altar of opportunities for humanos.

Ah hah! Here come the wayshowers. The flower-kissers, flower eagles, or some call them the humming-bird. They are ready. Mirror this upon jaguar magicians as you ascend. It is time to come out. The journey has been not so much of inviting in, it is an invitation for the divinity to come out from inside each humano. Indeed, it is the great coming out! Did you know Lola, it was a common phrase for the qweer, two-spirited jaguar magicians… to come out, to reveal their true selves. Then, let it be done. Come out! Everyone now! All there is… is love."

Together Ocelotl and Lola entered the ascension portal. The Phoenix, surrendered itself to ash and then dust before regenerating into a new form with new worlds to come and join those have already been.

www.ingramcontent.com/pod-product-compliance
Lightning Source LLC
Chambersburg PA
CBHW050743180526
45159CB00003B/1331